The Leaders Praise *Marketing Metrics in Action*

Wait a second . . . holding marketers accountable for their efforts? Applying metrics in a meaningful, results-oriented way? Making marketing understandable and process-based? Real take-aways in each chapter? Read this book, folks. Your business will be better for it.

—Joseph Carrabis, CRO and Founder, NextStage Evolution, LLC

Companies are demanding more from marketing—more data, more accountability, and more payoff. As the pressure increases, marketers need to develop the skills and utilize the resources necessary to improve their performance. *Metrics in Action* is an invaluable new resource that puts marketing metrics in the context of creating a performance-driven, accountable, and profit-generating marketing organization. Written for marketing professionals at all levels, *Metrics in Action* not only explains what they need to do, but shows them step by step how to do it.

—Mitchell Goozé, Former CEO Teledyne Components and author,
Value Acceleration

Whether you are a neophyte or a marketing leader, *Metrics in Action* has something for you. Use the guidance this important book offers to make your marketing efforts profoundly relevant to the business—and prove it!

—Steve Harriman, VP, Marketing NetQoS, Inc.

In *Marketing Metrics in Action*, Laura Patterson has provided marketers with an essential guide that will help them to be successful in their work. Drawing on her wide knowledge of marketing practices in major corporations, she points out that marketers today are measuring lots of things—but most of them are the wrong things! Much of what is being measured is not related to the essential business goals of the enterprise: market share, lifetime value and brand equity. In a book filled with contributions from key marketing executives in major corporations, Laura gives readers a priceless guide to selecting the right measurements that show, through dashboards, how marketing is contributing to the success of the business. Laura explains how marketing can work in cooperation with sales and finance to turn competition into collaboration resulting in a win-win situation for both. With this book, marketing can develop the metrics needed to create a culture of accountability for achieving the outcomes needed by top management. This book should be read by marketers in all major corporations.

—Arthur Middleton Hughes, Vice President /
Solutions Architect KnowledgeBase Marketing, and author of
Successful Email Marketing Strategies (Racom Books).

The need for Marketing to drive both strategy and execution has never been more acute. In asserting its responsibility to achieve profitable growth, Marketing must take the lead in driving integration and creating a common focus throughout an organization in order to demonstrate its value. Laura Patterson provides a vital framework for Marketing to garner the support of the C-suite and to build its leadership by helping achieve desired business outcomes and demonstrating performance in quantitative terms relative to those outcomes. If you want to understand how Marketing can be more effective, you've come to the right place!

—**Stuart Itkin, Former CMO, Kronos, Inc.**

Laura Patterson's book "Marketing Metrics in Action" is a genuine self-help book for marketers desperately trying to be relevant to their businesses. She tackles in a straightforward, checklist approach not only the "how" we should measure our activities, but the important "why." She pinpoints the key factors of success within marketing and gives suggestions for how to ensure that the entire organization from sales to finance understand marketing's contribution. A must read for any marketer who has had to answer the question — "so why do we need marketing?"

—**Theresa Kushner**
Director, Customer Intelligence, Strategic Marketing
Cisco Systems, Inc

"Laura Patterson does a wonderful job of articulating the foundations of effective marketing measurement. If you're thinking about how to move your marketing organization along a more productive path, you'll find this book very helpful."

—**Pat LaPointe, Managing Partner, Marketing NPV**

"Laura Patterson is the Emeril of Marketing Measurement - always kicking it up a notch. In her newest book, Laura provides practical advice and an easy-to-use benchmarking tool to help marketers improve the performance of their business unit, ultimately establishing marketing as the strategic, competitive advantage it is."

—**Christine Lowry, CMO, Athens Group**

Laura Patterson's deep, practical knowledge of marketing measurement shines from every page of this book. *Marketing Metrics in Action* goes beyond the usual lectures on why marketing metrics are important, to explain exactly how you can design, build and deploy a set of measures that will improve performance in your own organization—and advance your own career.

—**David M. Raab, Principal, Raab Associates Inc.**

Laura Patterson's journey in establishing marketing metrics is a valuable addition to the recent body of literature on the critical importance of greater accountability in marketing investments and actions. Instead of throwing her hands in the air and saying how difficult it is to measure marketing, she demystifies the area and provides essential tools that every company, large and small, can use to its benefit.

—Peter J. Rosenwald, Managing Partner, Consult Partners
Founder and President of Wunderman Worldwide and
former Chairman of Saatchi & Saatchi Direct
Author, *Accountable Marketing*

Eat less and exercise more. Every New Year's Eve, it's the same thing. Good advice and good intentions. A good idea—even with a good plan—is insufficient without a good measurement method to help monitor, encourage and communicate progress. In *Marketing Metrics in Action*, Laura Patterson combines years of first-hand experience and insight with some of the best thinking of our time to map out the philosophy, strategy and specific techniques for moving your marketing results from aspiration to computation.

This is not a book about data mining or predictive modeling. It's about managing by objective and measuring the impact of your marketing efforts. And it comes along just in time. As the economy grows weaker, having superior visibility into your marketing ROI is an absolute necessity. When the economy gets stronger, a rigorous marketing measurement capability is a significant competitive edge.

My advice? Eat less, exercise more, monitor how much you eat and exercise, and take the lessons of *Marketing Metrics in Action* to heart. You'll live longer, healthier and more profitably.

—Jim Sterne, Chairman, Web Analytics Association

Marketing Metrics in
Action

Creating a Performance-Driven
Marketing Organization

Laura Patterson

Foreword by Koen Pauwels

Editor: Richard Hagle
Cover and interior design by Sans Serif, Inc., Saline, MI

Published by:
Racom Books/Racom Communications
150 N. Michigan Ave.
Suite 2800
Chicago, IL 60601
312-494-0100 / 800-247-6553
www.racombooks.com

ISBN 13: 978-1-933199-15-3

Dedication

This book is dedicated to my father, David S. Tolpen, who as an artist and cartographer shared his talent for elegantly weaving together art and science in the pursuit of knowledge. His spirit continues to inspire me to seek answers to the never-ending questions asked by all children, "How?" and "Why?"

Contents

Acknowledgments

This book would not have been possible without the work, encouragement, and support of the following people:

- My husband **Mark Patterson**, who is kind and patient enough to encourage me in this and many other endeavors, even if it means less time spent with him.

- The **VisionEdge Marketing Team**, who performed the analytical and other work that informed the writing of this book, especially **Kathleen Feyh**, who provided copywriting and editing in order to ensure the book remained true to its mission.

- Contributors **Christopher Doran, Rick Kean, Jason McNamara, Michael Palmer, Koen Pauwels**, and **Roy Young**, whose words make this work ever more valuable to its readers.

- **Joseph Carrabis, Carol Kurimsky, Meg La Borde**, and **Breanna Rollings**, for their helpful input and suggestions throughout the writing and publishing process.

Foreword

Data is prolific but usually poorly digested, often irrelevant and some issues entirely lack the illumination of measurement.

John D.C. Little[1]

Still relevant decades later, Little's quote accentuates the tension between the abundance of market data at our disposal and the lack of actionable insights that derive from it. Recent surveys of marketing and non-marketing professionals consistently reveal increased expectations regarding marketing accountability. With their companies facing rapid change, powerful partners and fickle customers, chief marketing officers are challenged to both drive growth and to keep costs under control. In many leading companies this attention focuses on developing marketing metrics that are better aligned with business goals and on integrating them in a widely adopted and used dashboard. The first part of this process, to *Measure What Matters*, is the subject of ongoing business training—and the title of the first installment of this series.

The rub, as many early adopters have discovered, is in the second part of the equation. Even the best measurement devices fail to produce superior business performance if they are not widely used and incorporated in day-to-day decisions. To this end, a marketing dashboard should provide integration not just of data, but also of processes and perspectives throughout the organization. Such a dashboard bridges internal and external reporting by connecting inputs (activities) to outputs (firm performance), and provides executives in different departments and locations with a common lexicon for performance measurement and resource allocation. This book enables the reader to get this process started right: by involving stakeholders in key departments in building common ground, by assessing the current viewpoints, skills and tools and creating a culture of accountability in which managers act on, and are rewarded based on, these shared metrics.

In my research and teaching, translating metrics into action fits into the larger picture of how marketing should adapt in the face of increasing customer demands ("more for less"), proliferation of product lines, price challenges from emerging economies, channel power and media fragmentation. Indeed, the ability of marketing to reach across business functions to accomplish company goals is an increasingly important determinant of its success. Firms such as Coca-Cola have integrated marketing, innovation and strategic growth leadership into a single corporate function. Likewise, cross-national mergers and global expansion bring together departments with different values, performance metrics and reporting practices, necessitating a global consensus. Standardized tools and processes for effectiveness and efficiency are key characteristics of the "growth champions" among companies' marketing departments. In this regard, a dashboard helps ensure everyone is "on the same page" in order to detect and discuss marketing successes and failures.

According to leading CMOs, the ultimate metrics are "decision enablers" that combine a strong and actionable link to performance with forecasting accuracy. Google, for one, emphasizes the need to understand and quantify how metrics relate to each other. Unfortunately, most current dashboards do not go beyond tracking information, i.e., identifying metrics and populating them with historical data. The goal is to bridge this gap by identifying the leading indicators that have the largest long-term performance effects and by modeling their interactions to enable "what if" analyses and predict the impact of different decision options. However, better analysis and deeper insights do not suffice to help firms improve performance; they also need a higher degree of buy-in from managers at different organizational levels and from key functional areas. Key success factors include a strong fit between the supply (e.g., the dashboard's level of detail) and demand (e.g., the user's decision responsibilities), excellent inter-functional coordination, and users' trust that the dashboard will help them improve performance, instead of robbing them of their decision autonomy. In this regard, I believe dashboards should not just flag poor performance (the green light/red light system), but also exceptional performance (e.g., a blue light) and its causes. Such opportunities may then be fully exploited by scaling up investment in related activities and aligning the organization to fulfill the resulting demand growth. Far from extinguishing innovation and creativity, effective dashboards help marketing take smarter risks by assessing experimental projects and forecasting the profit potential of bigger, bolder initiatives.

This book represents a crucial stepping stone towards this brighter future. It provides excellent tools to assess where your organization is on the metrics continuum and how to move the needle in a given situation. Rich case studies demonstrate how companies actually use metrics to make more informed decisions that increase performance. At the same time, the frameworks and recommendations in this book are well grounded in marketing science and universal enough to apply across industries and firm strategy priorities. I particularly like the attention to implementation issues such as marketing-sales integration, marketing operations, mapping, selecting leading indicators and applying Six Sigma to marketing. The author, Laura Patterson, is ideally suited as your guide to these issues, having pioneered accountable marketing practices in companies like Motorola. Working closely with engineers, accountants and operations managers builds up a wealth of business insights, which she is happy to share and discuss with all of us. I wish you pleasant reading and a fruitful journey.

—Koen Pauwels
Amos Tuck School of Business
Dartmouth College
Hanover, New Hampshire

Note

[1] Little, J.D.C. (1970)"Models and Managers: The Concept of a Decision Calculus," *Management Science* 16(8): B466.

Preface

Creating a performance-driven marketing organization is a journey, one I've personally been taking for over thirty years. In my career I've had the pleasure of working with primarily two types of people: accountants and engineers. Embracing numbers was key to survival. My earliest days in marketing, back in the late 1970s, afforded me the opportunity to learn the concepts of customer lifetime value and share of wallet as key indicators for marketing. My then-employer, Dwight, was into customer relationship management long before the acronym CRM came into use. We had a filing system that would be the envy of any organization. We could locate customers by hobbies, anniversaries and birthdates, and services. And it was part of my job to develop programs that would motivate existing customers to buy additional services and to track those programs' success and return on investment.

After working for a few other organizations I ended up joining a small part of Motorola Semiconductor in Austin, Texas. Perhaps you are familiar with the notion of operations reviews: Motorola had elevated them to an art form. Each month the leadership team for the operation would meet and review all facets of the business. Initiatives being reviewed would be presented at the meeting. Now, presentations in those days were made using "foils," plastic sheets created by applying heat to a typed page that could then be shown on an overhead projector. At the end of your presentation, you handed over your foils. At this time I was in marketing, and most of my foils were about programs designed to secure new customers for our microcontroller chips. The operations manager would gather up all the foils and select a few to present at the next-level-up review, and so the process would go all the way up throughout the corporation. Over time I had the opportunity to sit in the back of the room and attend the meeting of the next level up, where my operations manager presented. And I noticed that not one of my foils was presented. Afterward, when I asked why, my manager was very straight with me. He said, "I'm an engineer, and I'm presenting to other engineers about how we're growing the business. While your foils are all very creative, with graphics for ads and information about campaigns and even expected response rates, et cetera, what my peers want to know is how this work is affecting the number of and rate of new design wins." The message was clear, and I renewed my focus on creating foils that would do just that.

At the same time, Six Sigma had become a mantra within the company. Every department and function was embracing measurability and accountability for continuous improvement. So I, with the help of our financial analyst and my manager, ultimately designed a set of marketing charts that we could use to determine what was and wasn't working and to help make decisions about the business. What we had developed was a dashboard and a set of performance indicators to create a performance-driven marketing organization.

I captured the first part of my journey toward making marketing performance-driven in *Measure What Matters: Reconnecting Marketing to Business Goals*, which is summarized in the first chapter of this book. This book tackles the second part of the journey. *Measure What Matters* identifies the first part: how the marketing function should align itself with three primary business outcomes (market share, customer value, and company equity) and identifies a dozen or so metrics that enable marketing to help business acquire, keep, and grow valuable customers and increase profitable revenue. *Metrics in Action* provides the second part: how marketing organizations can identify where they are on the metrics continuum and where they can yet go. It recommends a mapping process for forging the linkages between marketing and business outcomes and shows how to create a marketing performance dashboard and specifications for developing a quality dashboard. The book also discusses factors that will affect success in transforming marketing into a performance-driven organization, including relations with the C-suite, alignment with sales and finance, and the development of necessary processes, systems, tools, skills, and training. We hope you find the journey toward performance-driven marketing as rewarding as I have.

—Laura Patterson
Austin, Texas

Introduction to *Marketing Metrics in Action: Creating a Performance-Driven Marketing Organization*

Marketing accountability and measuring marketing performance are top issues on marketers' minds today. From the Association of National Advertisers to Frost & Sullivan and from IDC market research to the CMO (Chief Marketing Officer) Council, marketers' conferences and articles put marketing accountability front and center. The reason is that CEOs (Chief Executive Officers) want to understand how the funds marketing is investing on behalf of the company are contributing to the business; in other words, they are demanding more accountability from the marketing function. Guy Powell, Principal & Senior Consultant, of Demand ROMI, said it best when he said, "ROI is nothing without measurement."[1] While most marketers are measuring something, research indicates that there is room for improvement regarding metrics and their quality. Therefore, many companies are investing more resources, both people and money, into marketing performance measurement. According to the latest CMO Council survey, 53% of participating companies report that quantifying and measuring the value of marketing programs and investments is a key challenge for 2008, and 34% plan to deploy measures to track overall marketing ROI.[2] Also, a Measuring Marketing Performance study in October 2007 by the Aberdeen Group identified the top two pressures driving companies to develop new marketing performance measurement capabilities as the need to establish marketing's value to the organization and the need to improve management view into marketing decisions.[3]

Creating a performance-driven marketing organization—that is, one whose work moves the needle in key business outcomes and establishes marketing's value to the organization—will require new skills and capabilities. This explains why marketing organizations list customer analytics and strategic planning as key areas for staff recruitment and/or development in 2008.[4] Consider this from Elana Anderson, a former principal analyst at Forrester Research: "Marketing must improve its value to justify its existence as a centralized function."[5] Without developing quality metrics that communicate marketing's value, marketing may find its days as a stand alone department numbered, as it is absorbed into sales, finance, or other departments.

What Do We Mean by Performance Driven?

A performance-driven organization is one that promotes competition, maintains quality, and emphasizes a consistently high level of achievement.[6] To be performance driven is to set clear standards and align resources, policies, and practices that enable the organization to hit its targets. Performance-driven organizations are committed to understanding their achievements and failures in order to make ongoing adjustments to agreed-upon outcomes and to ensure continued excellence. They understand that being performance-driven is a process that begins with the development of a business plan and includes measurable and specific outcomes that enable the organization to develop performance measures. These organizations link their business and operational plans and focus on using data to improve fact-based decisions that will enable the organization to progress towards the attainment of its vision, mission, and objectives. They analyze performance at all levels—strategic, operational, and tactical—and institutionalize continuous improvements as a way to enhance decision-making and problem-solving, and to facilitate strategic direction. Performance-driven marketing organizations design their performance measurements to highlight achievements and reveal strategic and operational issues that hinder progress. These organizations define business metrics and KPIs (key performance indicators) for their business processes that are driven by business strategy and outcomes. Once they establish their measures, they use the metrics and KPIs to monitor and improve performance. Over time they gather enough data to create models and set up dashboards—tools they use to monitor both performance and process as part of the continuous improvement efforts.

Such an organization regularly applies the following management principles:

- Define clear standards.
- Articulate strategies that enable the organization to meet the defined standards.
- Align all resources, policies, and practices to carry out the articulated strategies.
- Track results.
- Use the data to drive continuous improvement and to hold the entire system accountable for performance.

Applying these management principles enables an organization to create a culture of commitment and accountability. A performance-driven organization, then, will have a set of measurable performance standards, a pointed focus on outcomes, and clear lines of accountability—all of which are important if a marketing organization wants to prove its value.

Where does your organization stand?

Performance measurement and management are essential for any organization to function effectively. Yet, many organizations try to function without the information they need to reward accomplishment or to identify issues that threaten their ability to perform. Many organizations use conceptual tools like the Balanced Scorecard as a framework for performance measurement. However, the Balanced Scorecard and similar tools do not provide a methodology for developing, implementing and maintaining a performance-driven organization. *This is the purpose of this book.* While there is no single performance measurement methodology that ensures a step-by-step, one-size-fits-all approach, this book attempts to outline the prerequisites, approaches, principles, stages, and integration strategies necessary to develop, implement and maintain a performance-driven marketing organization that supports the organization's mission and business outcomes. Performance-driven marketing organizations focus on creating initiatives that drive their objectives and strategies forward and design performance measurement systems that are objective, simple, quantifiable, and results-oriented. These organizations use their metrics to assess their performance in terms that are meaningful and relevant to their organizations. An organization doesn't become performance-driven overnight. There are varying degrees of being performance-driven, and we have identified four key stages: deficient, competent, proficient, and eminent. Take a moment to review these and determine which stage best reflects where your organization is.

Deficient: These marketing organizations do not have any defined processes or, if they do, their marketing processes are not documented. They have little or no measurement and few, if any, metrics. They rely on their internal experts to implement marketing programs that will work. These organizations are typically inefficient and tend to work from spreadsheets and project folders. They have little or no data, their data quality is suspect, and they are not held accountable for their results. They do not have any plans to deploy technology or develop processes.

Competent: Marketing organizations in this segment have established some basic rules related to processes and workflow. They are most likely measuring something, predominantly program results. They typically do not set performance targets for programs, do not have quantitative objectives, and cannot connect program data to business results. They place little or no emphasis on analytical skills and best practices. Their primary metrics are directed toward demand and lead generation. They recognize their limitations and generally think that technology is the fix. Thus these organizations are focused on technology that supports performance consistency and begins to capture data and to address data quality and integration.

Proficient: These marketing organizations are accomplished and skilled at data and measurement. Their performance is measured, reported, and visible. They have mastered marketing dashboards on all three levels: executive, operational, and functional. They have implemented technology that helps them systematically enhance key processes and facilitate operational efficiency. Their objectives are measurable, quantifiable, and linked to business outcomes, and they use measurement to set goals and performance targets. They are beginning to value analytics and analytical skills, and they may be establishing marketing operations capabilities and developing a marketing operations roadmap. They are beginning to explore best practices and to share their learning internally.

Eminent: These marketing organizations are exceptionally good at performance measurement and management. They have conquered analytics and incorporated best practices. They have evolved from using processes and data to focus on operational efficiency to leveraging these to improve strategic agility. Technology, process, measurement, and analytics are part of their corporate DNA. They live in a fact-based, data-driven environment where data is used to optimize marketing resources and test various scenarios. Metrics measure and evaluate the overall contribution marketing makes to their business.

What should you do right now if you recognize that your marketing organization is deficient in performance measurement and management? You should start by identifying an executive champion and creating a cross-functional team to transform the organization. This team should create a business case for performance measurement and management, define key processes focused on developing a measurable outcome-based marketing plan, require all programs have performance targets prior to approval and implementation, and articulate the measures that will determine success. The transformation will take time, so areas to be addressed need to be prioritized.

For those organizations that are competent and are looking to achieve proficiency, they most likely need someone who is process- and analytically inclined. These organizations need to automate their processes and use technology to help with data quality and integration. They must also begin to move from activity-based metrics to more operational and outcome-based metrics. These organizations will need to understand change management and to use change management processes to help the organization with the transformation.

It might seem that going from proficient to eminent would be an easy transition, but many organizations are content with being proficient and may feel that the effort required to become eminent may outweigh the payback. Performance-driven marketing organizations in the proficient category who want to reach eminence need to secure executive sponsorship in order to expand their scope and to secure resources to invest in modeling and real-time marketing automation. They will need to add scenario analysis allocation and marketing mix modeling to their capabilities. And they will ensure all of their personnel have the analytical capabilities to operate in this type of environment. These organizations work with human resources and finance to develop compensation packages that reward a culture of accountability.

Measuring Marketing: An Ongoing Conversation

The concept of measuring marketing has been around for a long time, yet our research has found that most companies fail to measure such things as cost to acquire, order value, share of wallet, churn rate, or brand equity, and other key business variables that marketing impacts. Rather, they measure such things as response rate, demo participation, event traffic, number of new contacts or leads, number of press hits, cost per lead, and lead aging. While the latter metrics offer some insight into the results of specific programs, they do not link marketing to business outcomes.

Perhaps the reason marketers have avoided the transition to outcome-based, performance-oriented metrics is because they view such metrics as "sticks" used by the C-suite to beat marketing into submission to sets of irrelevant quantitative standards. But quite the opposite is true. The metrics movement *empowers* marketing: Having reliable measurement data at hand allows marketers to come from a position of strength and gives them a basis from which to influence decision-making within the business. The ability to demonstrate how marketing affects business outcomes is necessary if marketing is to gain a seat at the executive table, instead of being marginalized within the company or absorbed into other business functions.

According to our own research, 93% of marketers at least attempt to measure marketing performance, though only 1 in 10 (10%) report that they do so effectively.[7] One major reason for the gap is that measurement can only move the needle for business if marketers are measuring the right things in the right ways efficiently, consistently, and accountably. Marketers need to know what to measure, how to measure it, and what they need to transform marketing into a performance-driven organization. This book attempts to fill the gap. It is a natural sequel to our first book, *Measure What Matters: Reconnecting Marketing to Business Goals*, which provided a way for organizations to begin measuring marketing and briefly discussed the elements of a dashboard. This book takes up where *Measure What Matters* left off by discussing key factors—from creating a culture of accountability to relations with the C-suite and other business functions and from the development of a marketing dashboard to identifying necessary tools, systems, skills, and training—needed to make marketing measurement performance-driven and successful in the long term.

Marketing Metrics in Action is divided into three sections. Each section discusses an aspect of creating a performance-driven marketing organization: the need for marketing to become more accountable, factors that contribute to success, and how to implement best practices.

Section I. The Case for Marketing Relevance

This section defines a performance driven organization. Chapter 1 provides a review of *Measure What Matters: Reconnecting Marketing to Business Goals*, which created the original framework for connecting marketing more quantitatively to the business by focusing on three key business outcomes that marketing affects: finding, keeping, and growing the value of customers. Key definitions such as *metrics* and *key performance indicators* are defined and used to demonstrate some of the tips in the book.

In Chapter 2 we take stock by discussing the state of measuring marketing today. Nearly all of the respondents from various studies realize the importance of measuring marketing and how it impacts senior management's confidence in their marketing personnel and programs. This chapter reviews some of the earlier research conducted in early 2005 by Forrester Research, Marketing Management Analytics, and the Association of National Advertisers and presents findings from more recent studies. The earlier studies found that 50% of respondents consider measurement to be the hardest part of marketing and that 51% are dissatisfied with how they measure marketing return on investment (ROI). This chapter looks at how far we've come.

According to Phil Kotler: "Marketing has the main responsibility for achieving profitable revenue growth for the company."[8] We do this by finding, keeping, and growing profitable customers. To become a performance-driven organization, marketing must shift its measurement priorities from focusing solely on tactically based metrics to including those that link it to customer acquisition, customer penetration, and growing customer value—the three responsibilities of marketing that squarely align it with nearly every organization's goals.

Most every company wants to be a dominant player in its market, however that market is defined. Most every company wants to retain its customers and increase their lifetime value. And ultimately, most every company—whether public or private—wants to increase its shareholder value. These three variables—market share, lifetime value, and brand equity—are what marketing affects and therefore must manage, monitor and measure. The more effective marketing's strategies and the better those strategies are executed, the more positive impact marketing can have on improving each of these outcomes and creating a performance-driven organization that moves the needle.

Section II. Key Success Factors

As anyone who has ever tried to instigate change in an organization knows, culture plays a key role. And as you will learn, culture plays a critical role in developing a performance-driven organization. In Chapter 3 we describe a culture of accountability and present a litmus test for marketing organizations to determine whether they possess a culture of accountability. The chapter outlines the steps for achieving a culture of accountability in order to align the work of marketing with the goals of the business in a measurable and effective manner.

Marketing is not an island. To be successful it must work and play well with other key parts of the organization, especially the leadership team and the sales organization. Chapter 4 explores how the role the CEO plays in enabling marketing to become a performance-driven organization. A marketing measurement initiative of any magnitude will need the blessing and support of the CEO. Marketing can be more successful when the CEO takes an active role in aligning the marketing function with the overall direction of the company. CEOs need to understand the role of marketing and how to measure marketing effectiveness beyond short-term incremental improvements in sales or campaign ROI. Even if marketing isn't a part of the CEO's day-to-day routine, the CEO needs to leverage his or her leadership role to make marketing performance-driven. Ten questions every CEO should ask when it comes to measuring marketing performance are posited in this chapter.

Chapter 5 examines how marketing can make an ally of Finance. For every business it comes down to economics–what the company must earn, what it must invest in order to achieve its goals, and whether it has made a good return on its investment. Marketers need to see themselves as members of the business team, as business unit owners who are making investments on behalf of the company. As a business unit owner, marketing is accountable for these investments, which means they must learn how to build relationships with the CFO. Any performance-driven marketing organization must learn and speak the language of business in order to surmount the distance between the marketing and finance functions and make finance an ally.

In addition to the leadership team, marketing must work with its partner in driving top line growth—the sales organization. When it comes to customer acquisition, these two organizations are two sides of the same coin, with marketing's job primarily being to increase the number of customers acquired faster and less expensively for the company that it would achieve by just adding more feet on the street. Any lack of alignment between these two functions can undermine the efforts of each. Chapter 6 discusses the obstacles faced in aligning marketing and sales and offers guidance in overcoming them. Key to this effort is the development of a common language and common metrics. In addition, we present a method for taking a customer-centric approach as a common basis in which both marketing and sales can participate as a way to foster alignment and positively impact the bottom line.

Key processes are needed to sustain a performance-driven marketing organization. Chapter 7 presents how the Six Sigma approach can serve as a tool for continuous improvement in marketing's strategic, tactical, and operational processes. We present how to use the DMAIC (Define-Measure-Analyze-Improve-Control) framework to create performance-driven marketing.

The performance-driven marketing organization needs someone to develop and own the processes and output, such as the dashboard, systems, tools, etc. Chapter 8 discusses the emergence and evolution of the marketing operations function. Here we define the role of marketing operations in the organization and describe steps for developing this function within existing corporations. Marketing opera-tions helps the marketing organization address the growing need for accountability and alignment among business functions.

Section III. From Ideas to Practice

We need ways to implement performance-driven marketing best practices. Other-wise, no amount of knowing *that* marketing needs to measure the right things the right ways in order to create value and communicate its contribution to business will bring us closer to *how*. In order to make the changes we've discussed so far rele-vant, we must return once more to metrics.

Chapter 9 introduces the metrics continuum and explains how marketers can use it in metrics initiatives. From activity-based measures alone to those that are outcome-based and linked to business goals, marketers can find out where they are on the continuum and where they can go to drive their efforts to greater levels of ef-fectiveness and efficiency through the use of relevant metrics and key performance indicators. Metrics and key performance indicators are critical elements in creating a performance-driven marketing organization because they provide focus and the means by which marketing can communicate its contribution to the company

Once you understand the metrics continuum, you need a way to determine which metrics you have and what you still need. Chapter 10 describes the process of conducting a metrics audit, so you can gain a clear picture of your current state and identify gaps that must be filled.

To be performance-driven means to commit to moving the needle for business. To do this, marketers must understand what business outcomes they need to affect and how to measure their impact on these outcomes. Chapter 11 shows how to use a mapping process to ensure linkage between business outcomes, key performance in-dicators, and marketing metrics.

With a clear picture of where you are now and where you need to go along the metrics continuum in order to make your marketing efforts more effective, you still need a way to implement your metrics goals and present the ways in which you're moving the needle for business. Chapter 12 discusses the characteristics of a quality metrics dashboard for tracking and reporting marketing performance, and the as-sessment standards and metrics that must be included on it. Here we provide an ex-ample dashboard specification that you can use to complete your own dashboard.

Initial attempts at measuring marketing performance often entail a manual process. In Chapter 13, contributing authors discuss what systems and tools are im-portant for any performance-driven marketing organization to have and use. They explain how marketers can identify what systems and tools they need from among those available, how they can acquire these tools and put these systems in place, and how to integrate them into marketing's work in order to move the needle effectively and accountably in business outcomes.

Finally, along with changes in culture, communication, and measurement methods, marketing needs to make sure its professionals have the skills and training they need to move the needle and communicate marketing's value to business. These include strong analytical skills and the ability to speak the language of business. In Chapter 14 contributing authors discuss what skills are necessary for making marketing performance-driven, how to assess current skill sets and gaps, where and how to acquire new skills and training, and what to expect as a result of training.

Marketing Metrics in Action is for anyone interested in taking the journey toward creating a performance-driven marketing organization, including marketers, C-suite executives, and professionals in other business functions who want to see marketing become more effective and accountable. From identifying the need for marketing to become more effective to explaining the factors and processes that can make that happen, each chapter of the book includes concrete steps your marketing organization can take to begin to move the needle for your company, no matter where you are now in the process of measuring marketing performance. Novice steps are realizable within 30 to 45 days; Intermediate steps are realizable within 45 to 90 days; Advanced steps vary in the time they require. Therefore, experts in marketing performance measurement should get as much out of *Metrics in Action* as those just now getting their feet wet by taking the concrete steps provided towards creating, developing, or improving their ability to move the needle effectively, consistently, and accountably for business.

Notes

[1] Henry Stewart (2008). Comments made regarding Guy Powell at DAM/MOM Symposium, New York, May 2008.

[2] CMO Council (2008). *Marketing Outlook.* <http://www.cmocouncil.org>

[3] Hatch, D. (2007). "Measuring Marketing Performance: The BI Roadmap to Information Nirvana." *Aberdeen.com* <http://www.aberdeen.com/summary/report/benchmark/4280-RA-measuring-marketing-performance.asp>

[4] CMO Council, *Marketing Outlook 2008.*

[5] Anderson, E. (2005). "Marketing needs to make its case quantitatively," *B to B*, May 2005.

[6] Crew, R. (1998). "Creating a Performance-Driven System," *FRBNY Economic Policy Review*, March 1998.

[7] VisionEdge Marketing, (2008). *2008 Marketing Performance Management Survey.* <http://www .visionedgemarketing.com>

[8] Kotler, P. (1999). *Kotler on Marketing.* New York: The Free Press, p. 18.

What We Need and Where We Are

This section sets the stage for creating a performance-driven marketing organization. A performance-driven organization establishes clear standards, aligns resources, policies, and practices than enable the organization to achieve its objectives. We recap the primary concepts in *Measure What Matters* and findings from our 2008 Marketing Performance Measurement and Management (MPMM) study and four-year trends. This information serves to remind us why we need the present book: Marketing performance is falling behind good intentions and best practices. First, while marketers recognize the importance of measurement, they have yet to invest in the tools and training that will enable them to do a better job of measuring. Second, marketing continues to measure all sorts of the things, but the C-Suite isn't convinced that they are measuring the *right* things and would like marketing to be able to quantify the financial value of its efforts. The sections following this one focus on how marketing can become more relevant and gain a permanent seat at the executive table.

1 Measure What Matters

Measure What Matters: Reconnecting Marketing to Business Goals (MWM) was one of the first marketing books designed to help business and marketing executives and professionals develop metrics that would enable them to demonstrate marketing's impact on the overall business. When the book came out in 2004, the drive for measuring marketing performance was already gaining momentum. A 2000 study by the Advertising Research Foundation had reported "enhanced return on marketing investment" to be one of the top priorities CEOs set for their marketing and research functions.[1] However, in the early part of the decade progress in measuring marketing performance was slow; a CMO Council survey of over 1,000 senior executives in 2004 revealed that 80% of the respondents remained unhappy with their ability to measure marketing performance—yet greater than 90% rated the measurement process as a high or moderate priority.[2]

VisionEdge Marketing had also begun its research on marketing performance measurement and management (MPM), and our results in the same time period yielded similar findings. Our work revealed that marketers were typically approaching metrics in one of two ways: starting from (1) financially related measures or (2) activity tracking. Neither of these metrics addressed long-term market position or provided the strategic insight necessary to outgrow and outpace the competition. Neither of these enabled marketing to show quantitatively its impact on business outcomes or how it was fulfilling its mission.

The Need for Better Metrics

The marketing discipline was ready. It demanded an approach and a set of metrics that relate marketing to the work it is expected to perform—finding, keeping, and growing profitable customers—and the outcomes these are expected to produce—customer acquisition, customer value, customer equity (Exhibit 1.1). *MWM* set out to provide businesses with a framework based on these three domains and an initial set of effective metrics linking marketing with these three business outcomes continuously identified as critical business objectives. These outcomes are: expanding the customer base, increasing sales from existing customers, and growing the value of existing customers.

The focus of the marketing profession was moved from measuring a never-end-

EXHIBIT 1.1 Marketing Metrics that Matter

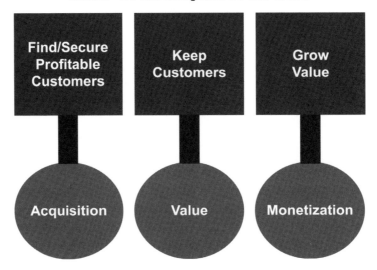

ing menu of items that consume a tremendous amount of energy, time, and resources to developing a set of metrics that show how marketing enables businesses
to realize desired outcomes. It provided a way for marketing to transition to what we
call Outcome-Based Metrics, adding to and improving the usual measurement of
marketing activities by providing targets for measurement and relevant ways to
measure marketing's impact on the achievement of business goals.

Marketing professionals had a new way to think about their work so that they
could present themselves as business people serious about business and connect
marketing with what business cares about: market share, lifetime value, and cus-
tomer/brand equity (Exhibit 1.2).

It defined key terms such as *metric, key performance indicator,* and *measurement.*
A metric is simply a numerical measure that represents a piece of business data. For
marketers a metric might be the number of qualified leads by week. A key performance indicator (KPI) is a metric that is tied to a target and that provides visibility
into performance. For example, fifty qualified leads per week at less than $250 per
lead. KPIs typically demonstrate the relationship between numbers, such as relating
the total marketing spend to the total qualified leads in order to provide the average
cost per qualified lead. The book also outlined a set of strategic metrics and key performance indicators that help achieve business goals, shifting the dialogue from activities to how marketing was moving the needle. This enabled marketing to link
strategy, investment and performance so the business could make better operational
and investment decisions.

The metrics in *MWM* were designed to enable marketing to maximize the value
of intangible assets—such as customers, channels, and the brand—and to focus

EXHIBIT 1.2 Objectives for Marketing

measurement efforts on those that would improve the business health of the organization, instead of simply monitoring a host of marketing activities, like attendance at trade shows, webinar attendees, number of press impressions, open rates, search engine rankings, and the like.

A New Approach to Measurement

Instead of starting with tactics, the measurement process should begin with outcomes and then define the marketing metrics that would best link to these outcomes, peeling the onion from the outside in. This approach tracked with such approaches as Integrated Marketing Communications, which emphasizes building a marketing communications plan from the outside-in rather than from the inside-out. Similarly, this approach to marketing metrics requires marketing to actively communicate and collaborate with other business functions—sales, accounting, contracts, services, etc—because that is the only way marketing could link its work to what mattered to the company.

The framework for metrics linked to business goals represented an initial taxonomy of 14 strategic metrics that would help determine which combination of drivers could be related to market share, value, and monetization (Exhibit 1.3). Each of these metrics was defined and then an approach was recommended for how to measure them.

EXHIBIT 1.3 Key Marketing Metrics

Market Share Indicators	Lifetime Value Indicators	Brand Equity Indicators
Share of Preference	Purchase Frequency	Price Premium
Share of Voice	Share of Wallet	Net Advocacy Score
Share of Distribution	Loyalty	Customer Franchise Value
Rate of Customer Acquisition	Tenure	New Product Acceptance Rates
Rate of Growth: Market		Product Margins

Where to Start Measuring

The basic message of *MWM* is that it is better to start the measurement process with small steps than not to start at all. Over the last few years, marketing performance management, marketing accountability, marketing metrics, and marketing dashboards have significantly evolved. Yet there are still many companies just beginning the journey. The parting advice in *MWM* still rings true: No company can tackle all of it right away. Therefore, we advised six metrics we still believe are the best place to start (Exhibit 1.4).

EXHIBIT 1.4 Where to Start: Six Marketing Metrics

Market Share & Performance Indicators	Lifetime Value & Performance Indicators	Brand Equity & Performance Indicators
• Share of Preference • Rate of Customer Acquisition	• Share of Wallet • Purchase Frequency/Recency	• Price Premium • Net Advocacy Score

We also introduced a set of categories that should be reflected on every dashboard shared at the executive level:

- New business metrics.
- Competitive metrics.
- Customer value metrics.
- Overall net advocacy score.
- Market value index.
- Product innovation.

Each of these should be reviewed in terms of effectiveness/impact, efficiency, and payback.

Marketing Metrics in Action takes up where *MWM* leaves off by describing and encouraging the development of a performance-driven marketing organization that can create and communicate value to business. It discusses how marketing organizations can identify where they are on the metrics continuum and where they can yet go, encourages the forging of linkages between marketing and business outcomes, and describes how to create a marketing performance dashboard and specifications for developing a quality dashboard. This book also discusses factors that will affect success in developing a performance-driven marketing organization, including relations with the C-suite, alignment with sales and finance, and the development of necessary systems, tools, skills, and training.

Summary: Six Steps You Can Take Tomorrow

1. **Stop Reporting on Activities to the C-suite:** Think in terms of what information is needed to make important strategic decisions. **Rather than the usual charts and activity status reports,** create a dashboard that shows how marketing is helping the organization acquire more customers, faster and less expensively, the incremental value marketing is having on the organization, and how marketing is growing the value of existing customers.

2. **Conduct an Audit:** Start with the data you have, define your gaps and your action plan to fill those gaps. Whether you do it yourself or hire a third party, take a proactive approach to finding out where your marketing organization stands when it comes to being performance driven and metrics savvy.

3. **Set your Goals:** Define 3 to 5 business outcomes that marketing drives, and identify the performance metrics that link marketing to these business results.

4. **Improve your Metrics Competency and Proficiency:** Recruit/train marketers with metrics skills, and invest in tools, systems, and processes. Assess the skills of your current staff and identify skills that need honing. Commit to at least one in-house training program that is designed to "get" all of your staff on the path to creating a performance-driven marketing organization.

5. **Use Metrics to Guide Business Decisions:** The purpose of measuring performance should ultimately be to ascertain what is and isn't working. This way marketing teams prioritize and (if necessary) redeploy efforts and resources, and adjust strategies and tactics. The metrics you choose should facilitate the process of making appropriate adjustments with some confidence in how those adjustments will affect results.

6. **Foster a Culture of Accountability:** Make "a personal choice to demonstrate ownership for achieving desired results" (Connors and Smith, 2004). Assess your current culture and put processes, systems, tools, compensation, and infrastructure in place within the year that will create a performance-driven culture.

Notes

[1] Cook, W.A. and V. S. Talluri (2004). "How the Pursuit of ROMI Is Changing Marketing Management," *Journal of Advertising Research*, Vol. 44, Issue 3.

[2] CMO Council (2004). "Measures and Metrics: The CMO Council Marketing Performance Measurement," *MPM Report*. <http://www.cmocouncil.org>

The State of Measuring Marketing

The increasing number of marketing performance management (MPM) and marketing measurement attests to the increased concern about marketing accountability. For example, the results of VEM studies conducted over the past seven years have often been corroborated by other research conducted by the ANA (Association of National Advertisers), Forrester, the CMO Council, and Deloitte, to name a few. Between the release of VEM's 2007 and 2008 studies, the ANA and MMA (Marketing Management Analytics) announced the findings from their fourth annual Marketing Accountability Study.[1] One of their key findings was the need for greater alignment between marketing and finance, which we discuss in detail in Chapter 5. Of particular note is that while almost all companies (92%) have created some type of marketing accountability process, more than half of marketing executives are noticeably dissatisfied with marketing accountability. Programs have proliferated, but dissatisfaction reigns. And the frustration levels among company executives are rising: Dissatisfaction with marketing ROI (return on investment) measurements, lack of marketing ROI definitions, and poor organizational response to marketing ROI data are top sources of their frustration.

Even though marketing professionals have been beating the drum about aligning marketing with business outcomes, only 55% of marketers indicated that their marketing ROI goals were closely aligned with their company's overall corporate goals. By contrast, half (51%) said there were no written goals for marketing ROI in their organizations. Rather, marketers commonly used other measures to track effectiveness, metrics that do not aid in demonstrating how well marketing is moving the needle for the business. Note that while 70% of respondents cited "return on objective" as an important measure, only 36% were using that as a metric.

VisionEdge Marketing's annual Marketing Performance Management and Measurement (MPM) survey shows similar findings.[2] Two themes are very clear in the results of the 2008 survey:

1. Marketing is expected to demonstrate the value it contributes.
2. Marketing is expected to calculate payback for the money it invests on behalf of the company.

In order for marketing to achieve these expectations, marketers need to understand business outcomes and their role in enabling their organizations to realize these outcomes.

It is more evident in the 2008 study than in years past that marketers do indeed understand what is expected of them. There is an important gap, however, that continues to exist between expectations and behavior. The 2008 survey findings reveal that marketers are faced with a series of disconnects—between priorities and intentions, on the one hand, and actions and abilities on the other. Until marketers bridge these gaps, marketing will continue to find it difficult to articulate its value and demonstrate its impact. And the trend will continue that, as the survey results show, marketing is seen as marginally effective at measuring its contribution to the overall business, especially in financial terms. Four key disconnects emerge upon reviewing the results of the 2008 Marketing survey.

Disconnect #1:
Marketing Plans Still Not Aligned with Business Goals

While marketing *expectations* are finally becoming aligned with business goals, marketing *plans* are not. Marketers indicate they understand what is expected of them, but they are not quite putting those expectations into practice. For example, with the exception of market share, the performance indicators featured in most marketing plans are not tied to larger business goals , but are focused more on short-term or incremental measures (Exhibits 2.1 and 2.2). This is one of the sources of the gap between expectations and action that continues to impede marketers' ability to demonstrate their value to business.

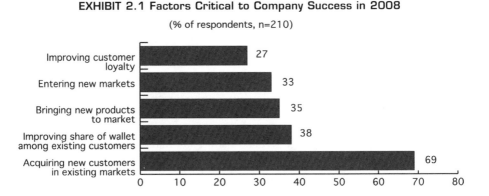

EXHIBIT 2.1 Factors Critical to Company Success in 2008

(% of respondents, n=210)

Factor	%
Improving customer loyalty	27
Entering new markets	33
Bringing new products to market	35
Improving share of wallet among existing customers	38
Acquiring new customers in existing markets	69

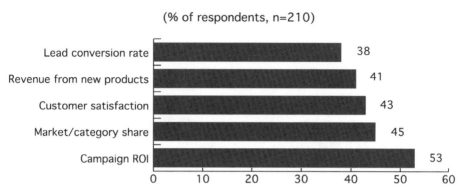

EXHIBIT 2.2 Marketing Plan Key Indicators of Performance

(% of respondents, n=210)

Disconnect #2: Metrics Don't Match Expectations

Marketing understands that it is expected to track and measure indicators tied to increased profitability, yet the metrics that marketers use do not reflect this expectation. Related to, but separate from, the misalignment of marketing plans and business goals, this is the second source of the gap between expectations and results. This discrepancy is particularly noticeable when looking at the top two business and marketing priorities, increasing share in existing markets and increasing share among existing customers. Marketers are not proactively tracking market share; nor are they tracking and reporting those metrics most closely associated with these two priorities. Market share metrics that are falling by the wayside include:

- rate of customer acquisition.
- share of distribution.
- share of voice.
- share of preference.

And while customer loyalty metrics are being tracked, other existing customer metrics are being neglected, including:

- purchase frequency/recency.
- customer lifetime value.
- length of customer tenure.
- share of wallet.

EXHIBIT 2.3 Measuring What Matters: Market Share Metrics

(% of respondents, n=210)

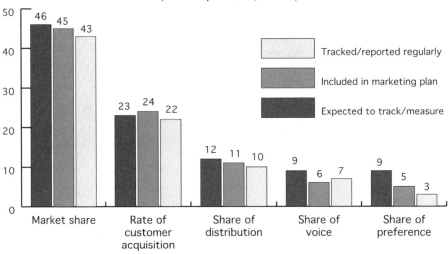

EXHIBIT 2.4 Measuring What Matters: Existing Customer Metrics

(% of respondents, n=210)

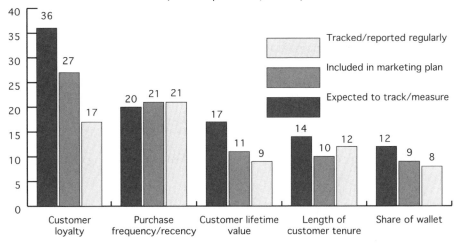

Disconnect #3: Intentions and Investments Out of Sync

Respondents list a lack of internal processes or coordination of internal processes (33%) and a lack of data or tools to acquire the necessary data (29%) as their greatest challenges to improving marketing performance (Exhibit 2.5). Even though respondents realize they need to make these changes, they are not making the investment necessary in order to do so: Only a third (36%) have a budget set aside to train their personnel in how to track and improve marketing performance (Exhibit 2.6):

EXHIBIT 2.5 Top Challenges to Improving Marketing Effectiveness

(% of respondents, n=210)

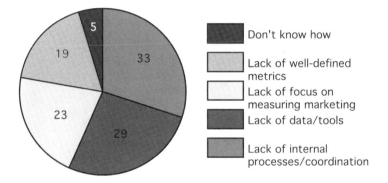

Don't know how

Lack of well-defined metrics

Lack of focus on measuring marketing

Lack of data/tools

Lack of internal processes/coordination

EXHIBIT 2.6 Budget Set Aside for MPM Training

(% of respondents, n=210)

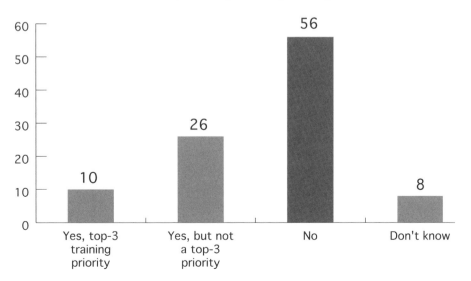

Disconnect #4: Best Practices Still Elusive

An overwhelming majority (85%) assert that it is important to stay abreast of MPM
best practices, yet most do not do any best practice benchmarking. Too many (39%)
fail to audit and benchmark their metrics regularly, and fewer than half (44%) plan
to do so this year. By failing to set benchmarks and neglecting to audit their metrics
regularly, marketers lose their ability to assess and improve their performance in
helping achieve their goals of acquiring, retaining, and growing valuable customers.

EXHIBIT 2.7 Staying Abreast of MPM Best Practices Is Important

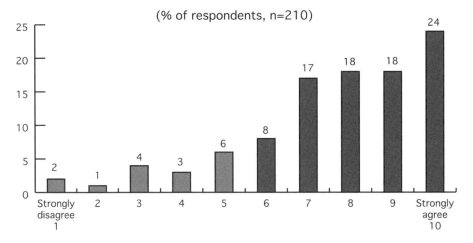

EXHIBIT 2.8 Frequency of Metrics Auditing/Benchmarking

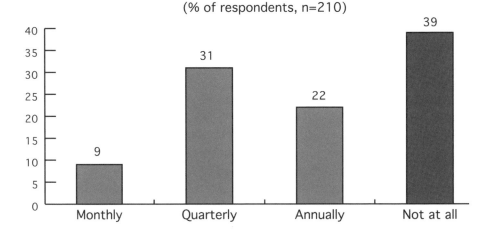

The Pattern of Trends

Unfortunately, none of this is new. The findings of our 2008 survey are a culmination of trends we've seen during the seven years that we have conducted the survey. To wit, marketers are aware that business expects them to be able to measure and report on marketing's impact and value. Yet, they remain challenged in their ability to do so, even with the proliferation in recent years of resources and best practices. The challenges marketers face are a result of four primary disconnects that result in a gap between expectations and performance:

- misalignment of marketing plans with business goals.
- misalignment of metrics with expectations.
- investments not matching intentions.
- best practices continuing to elude most marketers.

In order to close the gap, marketers understand they need to do a better job of aligning marketing plans with business goals and then following through on those plans with the right metrics. Marketing must establish and track metrics that provide a clear picture of its contribution to business, including important market share and existing customer metrics. In addition, marketers need to audit and benchmark

Move the Needle

	Novice: Gain clarity as to the business outcomes for your organization and marketing's role in relation to each of these outcomes. Don't settle for vague outcomes like "Increase market share." Instead, make sure the outcomes are specific enough that it is clear how the needle needs to move. For example, "Double the number of large-company customers in each growth market," or "Retain >50% of tier-1 customers in all markets." You should align all marketing objectives with these specific outcomes.
	Intermediate: Establish performance targets for every marketing objective. Have quantifiable objectives tied to each business outcome, as opposed to objectives that are basically activities.
	Advanced: Benchmark performance indicators relevant to your industry. Based on the benchmarking, develop a set of key performance indicators for your marketing organization.

their metrics regularly, if they want to be able to assess their current performance and chart trajectories for improvement.

Finally, improvement in marketing performance and measurement capabilities doesn't come by wishing it were so. Marketers are going to need to invest in skills, analytics, and processes if they want to be able to demonstrate their accountability and improve their ability to measure. These steps are essential for marketing to measure and report its value and relevance to business. In the next sections of this book we outline factors that will help marketing succeed in becoming more performance-driven and in demonstrating its value to business.

Notes

[1] Association of National Advertisers, and Marketing Management Analytics, Inc. (2007). *2007 Marketing Accountability Survey*, presented at the ANA Marketing Accountability Forum, September 10, 2007.

[2] VisionEdge Marketing (2008). *VisionEdge Marketing Marketing Performance Management Survey*. <http://www.visionedgemarketing.com>

SECTION II

Key Factors for Success

It takes more than an understanding of the current situation to implement the changes marketing needs to undergo in order to become a performance-driven organization. Other factors, such as corporate culture, business function alignment, and C-suite guidance and participation, play a key role in improving marketing performance and increasing its contribution to the business. A culture of accountability helps align marketing with business goals measurably and effectively, and the CEO cannot stand separate from the development of such a culture. Finance and sales have much to contribute to and gain from performance-driven marketing, so it is best to have these functions as fellow travelers on the journey to improved marketing performance.

Continuous improvement can be ensured by the application of Six Sigma to marketing, and a new business function, Marketing Operations, helps bring it all—culture, alignment, and improvement—together into an effective and quantifiable whole.

Creating a Culture of Accountability

The increasing complexity of marketing is a key driver behind marketing performance measurement and management. Today's marketers must navigate a growing number of challenges. The number of messages customers are exposed to continues to increase, customers are asserting more control over how they want to receive information and be contacted, and marketing is facing more regulation than ever before with efforts such as the do-not-call list and the CAN-SPAM Act. In addition, global competition is continuously putting pressure on companies' profit margins, placing marketing budgets under ever more scrutiny.

As a result of these challenges, today's marketers must implement a performance measurement culture within their organizations to maximize efficiency, streamline communications, ensure that customer preferences are adhered to, and optimize budgets. Creating a performance-driven marketing culture begins with clearly articulated goals and objectives and with well-defined metrics that will be used to measure performance. Clear definition of goals helps everyone in the organization understand the value and purpose of a performance-driven organization. Alignment across roles provides each team member and the organization as a whole with the ability to measure progress against key objectives. And, along with clear goals and alignment, the creation of a successful performance-driven organization requires people, processes, and technology.

More often than not, marketing remains the only organization within an enterprise that relies on subjective criteria, rather than performance metrics aligned to business outcomes, to determine success. Other organizations have processes and measures in place that tell them when business objectives have been met. For instance, sales knows to the penny whether they made their year-end quotas; engineering understands precisely whether a manufacturing release was completed on schedule and to specifications; and IT can report its work-order closure rate at any time. Marketing, however good its intentions, usually lacks similar yardsticks to those used by other business functions. According to Booz Allen Hamilton and the ANA, a majority of CEOs say the greatest need within marketing is more analytics.[1]

Key Challenges

One of the key challenges to creating a culture of accountability is marketing leadership. In a joint study, researchers from Forrester Research and Heidrick & Struggles asked 122 chief and senior marketers their top marketing objectives from a pre-defined list. Improving marketing ROI was among the top four.[2]

Creating a culture of accountability starts at the top. Sadly, though, many chief marketing officers do not see the analytical skills that are critical to measurement as being critical to their success. For the 122 chief and senior marketers in the Forrester study, collaboration, analytical skills, and budget and resource management—all key skills for creating a performance-driven organization—didn't make the list when CMOs were asked to identify the five skills that they felt are the most important to success. To create a culture of accountability, the marketing leadership is going to have to step up to the plate.

Defining a Culture of Accountability

To answer this question we must define both *culture* and *accountability*. *Webster's Dictionary* defines culture as "the set of shared attitudes, values, goals, and practices that characterizes an institution or organization."[3] According to Kotter and Heskett, corporate culture is "an interdependent set of values and ways of behaving that are common to a community and tend to perpetuate themselves."[4] Put another way, culture comprises a set of shared values, beliefs, and behavioral norms that guide conduct or predict outcome. Culture is an important element for any organization. It conveys a sense of identity and establishes social stability. Given culture's essential role in governing conduct, it is certainly the vehicle for bringing accountability into marketing.

Webster's Dictionary defines accountability as "an obligation or willingness to accept responsibility or to account for one's actions."[5] However, Connors and Smith provide a more useful definition in terms of accountability in relationship to business: "a personal choice that reflects a sense of ownership for where things are headed."[6] As marketers, we are certainly accountable for the actions we take on behalf of our businesses. We must now make a personal choice to account for the results we achieve from those actions. Through our personal choices and ownership, we contribute to creating a culture of accountability for the marketing function and our organizations.

Using these definitions of culture and accountability, we can define a culture of accountability as a shared set of behavioral norms grounded in the belief that individuals—and by extension the groups they belong to—are responsible for their actions as well as the results they achieve. Remember that a performance-driven organization is one that promotes competition, maintains quality, and emphasizes a high level of achievement. Accountability is required at every step, and its norms must be built into and guide the development of standards and strategies, the alignment of resources and policies, and the tracking and use of data for driving improvement.

In 2005, the American Marketing Association created a definition for marketing accountability that captures the essence of these ideas: "The responsibility for the systematic management of marketing resources and processes to achieve measurable gains in return on marketing investment and increased marketing efficiency, while maintaining quality and increasing the value of the corporation."[7] This definition highlights some of the key elements the marketing discipline would need to embrace, such as systematic management practices and processes, measurability in terms of ROI, efficiency, and effectiveness. Yet the demand for more accountability for the money companies invests in marketing takes more than just process and analytics; it takes a performance-driven organization. And a key characteristic of a performance-driven organization is a culture of accountability.

How Culture, Leadership and Performance Are Linked

Klein, Masi, and Weidner discuss the impact of culture on performance, finding that cultures that encourage teamwork, employee development, and empowerment achieve higher quality outcomes, higher quality results.[8] Culture is clearly a key ingredient of performance. The ultimate objective for creating a culture of accountability is to enable an organization to achieve superior long-term performance. It's a chicken and egg thing. The lack of performance measurement in marketing suggests a lack of accountability. And where a culture of accountability is lacking, marketing cannot focus on measurement and performance.

Is it true that when it comes to marketing, we're missing the mark on measuring our performance? Various studies, including one conducted by VEM and one conducted by the CMO Council in 2008, show that more than 56% of executives and marketing professionals are dissatisfied with their ability to demonstrate the value of marketing, with 21% not making any progress at all on this front. Will it matter if we address culture? Companies with a culture of accountability have formal and comprehensive marketing performance management systems. And research has found that companies with such systems routinely outperform companies without them, experiencing 29% higher sales growth, 32% higher market share, and 37% greater profitability.

Clearly, we need to create a culture of accountability for marketing if marketing is going to become performance driven. We find that a culture of accountability for marketing consists of three core attributes:

1. Shared Knowledge: Everyone in the marketing organization needs to have clear visibility into the organization's purpose, including performance targets, timelines, measurement, and consequences.

2. Alignment: Every single marketing objective should be linked directly to a business outcome.

3. Belief: The people within marketing must have an unwavering belief in the essential value of measuring, evaluating, and improving their work based upon objective criteria, linking performance and accountability.

Identifying a Performance-Driven Culture of Accountability

There is a four-part litmus test any organization can use to see if it has the "right stuff." First, marketing must define specific goals with measurable criteria to achieve clear results that will impact the business. Second, each person in marketing must assume accountability for the ultimate business outcome, not just for his or her individual tasks. Third, there must be a focus on achieving results beyond the boundaries of each individual's job. And, fourth, each person within the marketing organization must know how his or her job advances corporate and marketing goals. That is, each person must focus on outcomes rather than tasks (updating the web site, creating and implementing a campaign, revising the pricing model, etc.).

Does your marketing group pass the test? Is it aligned with and integrated into the corporation? If not, here are four steps to help your marketing team develop a culture of accountability:

1. Defining and creating the culture.
2. Auditing the existing state of affairs.
3. Implementing, measuring, and revising new cultural norms and accountability.
4. Rewarding your team for the changes.

Defining and Creating the Culture

Defining and creating a culture of accountability takes leadership, time, and compensatory alignment. Leaders in the C-suite drive culture and cultural change in the corporation. The marketing leadership is similarly responsible for creating or changing the culture of the marketing organization. Leadership enables the transformation by endorsing, exhibiting, and promoting behaviors that model the desired culture. They lead by example. Changing a culture takes time because it essentially involves developing and implementing new business processes. Anyone who has been involved with creating, executing, and integrating a new business process knows that such changes can take months, even years. Besides leadership and time, performance is tied to how people are compensated. Compensation reinforces the culture. Organizations with cultures of accountability closely align their compensation structures with performance.

An audit comes next. The existing state of affairs must be assessed to determine what must change and where gaps exist. In addition to providing valuable insight into culture, audits help an organization determine the skill levels, effectiveness, and efficiency of the marketing function. You can conduct your own audit, or you can use an objective third party with expertise in marketing performance management. Regardless of what you choose, securing a sense of where you are is an important step in determining where you need to go, which we discuss in greater detail in Chapter 10 of this book.

Then you must implement, measure, and revise your new cultural norms and accountability. While the top three issues marketers are expected to address are increasing share in existing markets, increasing share of business with existing customers, and growing the company's brand value, many do not have processes in place to track performance in these areas.[9] Developing such processes enables a culture of accountability and demonstrates the existence of such a culture.

The planning process gives us an ideal opportunity to make progress. Producing a plan provides the means to include performance metrics and integrate accountability. Performance metrics need to focus on the long-term success of the organization, not just this quarter's or this year's activities. A marketing plan must be a strategy for how marketing is going to move the needle and account for the money invested in it, the resources it uses, and the decisions it makes. Susan Annunzio, author of *Contagious Success*, reminds us that "the single biggest impediment to high performance around the world is short-term thinking."[10]

Finally, there must be some reward for making the necessary changes. Adherence to the processes and participation in a culture of accountability must be re-

Move the Needle

Steps You Can Take Tomorrow to Create a Culture of Accountability

	Novice: Put your marketing team to the accountability litmus test. Identify at least one area for improvement and develop an action plan to address this area.
	Intermediate: Schedule meetings with key business functions to discuss marketing accountability and what sales, finance, and the C-suite want to see from marketing. Develop a mutual documented contract that will enable marketing to achieve new standards of performance.
	Advanced: Allocate budget and commit to conducting a marketing performance audit. Communicate the results of the audit and use it to address processes, skills and infrastructure improvements.

warded. One way is through aligning compensation with performance within the new cultural norms.

Creating a culture of accountability is a journey. It is a vital one, though, because a performance-driven organization cannot exist without a supporting culture, and a marketing organization that is not proactively accountable cannot possibly demonstrate its contribution to the enterprise. The journey begins by taking accountability and performance seriously. To complete the journey you will need to redefine the rules of the game for your organization. At the end of the journey stands the opportunity for marketing professionals to take their rightful place at the leadership table by accounting for the investments they make on behalf of their organizations and demonstrating their value to the business.

Notes

[1] ANA and Booz Allen Hamilton (2004). "Are CMOs Irrelevant? Organization, Value, Accountability, and the New Marketing Agenda." *BoozAllen .com.* <http://www.boozallen.com /media/file /143264.pdf>

[2] Forrester Research, Inc. and Heidrick & Struggles International (2007). "The Evolved CMO." *Forrester.com.* <http://www.forrester.com/evolvedcmo>

[3] Merriam-Webster (2008). "Culture (definition)." *Merriam-Webster Online.* <http://www.merriam-webster.com /dictionary/culture>

[4] Kotter, J.P. and J.L. Heskett (1992). *Corporate Culture and Performance-* New York: The Free Press:141.

[5] Merriam-Webster (2008). "Accountability (definition)." *Merriam-Webster Online.* <http://www.merriam-webster.com /dictionary/accountability>

[6] Connors, R. and T. Smith (1999). *Journey to the Emerald City.* New York: Prentice Hall Press: 38.

[7] American Marketing Association (2006). "Marketing Accountability Study White Paper." *MarketingPower.com* <http://www.marketingpower .com/search.php?SearchFor =marketing+accountability &Session_ID=d 2947d8944516dec1dbe6ec8f82cb4f6&Type=0>

[8] Klein, A.S., R.J. Masi, and C.K. Weidner (1995). "Organization culture, distribution and amount of control, and perceptions of quality." *Group and Organization Management,* Vol. 20(2):122–148.

[9] VisionEdge Marketing (2008). *VisionEdge Marketing Marketing Performance Management Survey.* <http://www.visionedgemarketing.com>

[10] Annunzio, S. (2004). *Contagious Success: Spreading High Performance throughout Your Organization.* New York: Penguin Group: 17.

Ten Questions Every CEO Should Ask about Measuring Marketing

Today, CEOs have so many things to address that they often lack the time to focus on marketing challenges, delegating them instead to the marketing organization. Yet increased competition, successfully bringing new products to market, and a renewed focus on customer engagement are making marketing increasingly important to corporate success. It is just as important for marketing to be on the CEO's radar screen as compliance, inventory management, and reengineering, especially given the continued investments many companies are making in business intelligence and customer relationship management.

We exist in a market where brands can emerge and topple almost overnight. Driving profitable revenue growth, conducting market and customer research, gathering competitive intelligence, defining new products and services, and identifying new market opportunities are the domain of marketing and primarily the responsibility of the CMO.

Study after study suggests that many marketing functions are not in sync with companies' overall strategy. The impact of this lack of alignment on business is significant. Companies are experiencing a gap between actual revenue growth and investors' expectations. If the gap persists, the result can be lower margins, loss of market share, slowing growth, and defecting customers. Therefore the CEO must also take an active leadership role to insure that the marketing department within the organization has the skills and resources necessary to address the challenges and opportunities of the market in order to produce the desired business results.

Most every CEO would like marketing to do a better job of aligning the marketing organization with the business' agenda. They want marketing to be performance driven and linked clearly to business priorities and outcomes. CEOs do not need to be marketing experts, but they do need to have a clear understanding of the role of marketing and of how to measure marketing effectiveness beyond short-term incremental improvements in sales or campaign ROI. Even if marketing isn't a part of the CEO's day-to-day routine, s/he needs to leverage his or her leadership role for marketing. While CEOs should delegate strategic implementation and tactical decisions related to product, price, placement, and promotion to the CMO, it is the CEO's job to make sure the marketing organization's strategy and plan support the company's greater strategic goals. With guidance from the CEO, marketing can closely focus its activities on initiatives that generate profitable relationships.

Marketing that isn't aligned with the overall business objectives is a recipe for a myriad of business ailments. Only by aligning marketing with the strategies of both the corporate and business unit levels and fostering collaboration between marketing and the rest of the organization can a business develop a set of metrics that will measure marketing's impact. CEOs can help implement and encourage the necessary collaboration across business functions that will ultimately improve marketing performance.

In our work with over 100 companies, many CEOs tell us they want marketing to focus on top line growth, enable the organization to respond quickly to market dynamics and changing customer requirements, and stimulate innovation. What they say they see, however, is a marketing organization more focused on image and identity, tactical execution in terms of marketing activities supporting events, lead development, etc. We hear CEOs tell us regularly that, rather than focusing tactical issues and reporting on response rates, leads generated, event traffic, and other activities, they would like to understand how marketing is driving growth, developing metrics that demonstrate how marketing is contributing to both the top and bottom lines. A bottom-up approach to marketing accountability and metrics will fail without direction from the top. If a CEO wants marketing to measure and convey its value in the same language and metrics used by the business, the CEO needs to be sure the marketing organization has the tools, systems, and skills to do the job.

Being able to keep pace with the rapidly changing market and to capitalize on new growth opportunities requires a new set of marketing skills, particularly in the area of analytics. When we ask CEOs whether there is a clear contract with the CMO or VP of Marketing regarding expectations and resources committed to improving marketing's measurement capabilities and market and customer insights, they often admit this isn't on the top of their agenda. For performance-driven marketing to succeed, the CEO has to see these as priorities and support them.

The CEO's definition of marketing success must be clear to his or her marketing people. There are so many things that can be measured, but only a few really matter to the business. It's easy to think that just because something has a number attached to it, it is a metric. Having metrics is one thing; having the right set is another. Marketing can collect all sorts of marketing-performance metrics, from customer satisfaction to retention, and from brand awareness to pipeline contribution. The CEO should make sure the marketing metrics suggested by marketing leadership truly provide insight into how marketing is supporting the business' goals. Prior to any plan being created and implemented, the CEO and marketing team should agree on the performance indicators that will be used to correlate marketing's impact on business outcomes. It's important to decide at the start which metrics and key performance indicators will have the most impact and then to track progress to these.

For the metrics to be right, they need to tie back to the business outcomes and purpose of marketing: driving top-line growth and profitable revenue.

Think of these performance indicators as essentially a contract between marketing and the executive team. As such they should be based on strategies designed to create a positive experience between your targets/customers and your company/offer that will facilitate customers sticking with your company even in times of competitive pressure or adversity and developing a preference to buy and use your products/services. The performance indicators demonstrate how well marketing understands the needs of different customer segments, which channels to deploy to customers make buying decisions, and how to create preference for your company and its products and services. And it may not just be a question of measuring; additional marketing capabilities may be required. Almost 75% of the chief marketers polled at a recent CMO summit organized by the Marketing Science Institute and McKinsey agreed that the skills they needed were becoming so specialized that their organizations would have to operate quite differently in the future. The changing environment calls for new marketing capabilities, both in the marketing organization and within the company.

To ensure the marketing organization is aligned with the business, measuring the right things and that the organization has the right skill sets, here are 10 initial questions every CEO should ask their marketing leadership:

1. How are our customers' needs evolving and what resources are our customers using to make buying decisions?
2. Which customer segments offer us the best opportunities and what marketing strategies do you recommend we deploy to take advantage of these opportunities?
3. Where can we gain a competitive advantage?
4. What business outcomes will marketing directly impact?
5. What marketing factors can make the greatest material contribution to our deal and revenue targets?
6. What metrics and key performance indicators will you present to show this impact?
7. How do you plan to foster collaboration between your marketing team, the sales organization, product organization, and business units?
8. What information will you need to measure your impact?
9. What systems, tools, processes, analytical and data management skills will you need to add to improve your measurement capabilities?
10. What investments does the company need to make to improve marketing's ability to measure its contribution?

Satisfactory answers to these types of questions should help insure the marketing leadership is on the right track to being able to assess its contribution to the corporation. The answers will help establish what metrics best measure marketing's impact as well as enable everyone on the leadership team to make marketing decisions that positively impact the business.

Move the Needle

CEOs Get Involved in Marketing Performance Management

	Novice: The CEO should meet with the marketing team to reach agreement on the business outcomes that marketing must impact and how this impact will be measured. The objective of this meeting is to make sure marketing activities and investments are aligned with measurable objectives and business outcomes. Following the meeting, the marketing team should establish performance targets for every objective.
	Intermediate: The CEO should meet with the CMO and marketing team to agree on a set of key performance indicators to measure marketing's contribution. At this meeting the CEO should define, and the marketing team implement, a test-measure-reflect process for every marketing initiative.
	Advanced: The marketing organization should evaluate and recommend for implementation systems and tools that enable them to capture marketing performance in real time. The CEO and leadership team must support and encourage the purchase of necessary technologies. With these systems in place, the marketing organization should track data that can be used to create leading indicators.

Finance:
From Adversaries
to Allies

Global competition, commoditization, market fragmentation, and Sarbanes-Oxley have all converged to create an environment that requires companies to create better processes, address controls, and assess risk. In addition, zero-based budgeting has become the norm. This convergence marks a new age for marketing in the 21st century, the Age of Accountability. This new age forces marketers to change our focus from awareness and image to business outcomes such as revenue, customers, cash flow, and shareholder value. Marketing organizations are sitting squarely in the sites of the finance organization.

The 2007 results of the ANA/MMA (Association of National Advertisers/Marketing Management Analytics) study on marketing accountability suggest that marketing has a considerable way to go when it comes to its relationship with finance.[1] The study found that the relationship between marketing and finance still lacks strength and consistency—particularly when attempting to establish metrics and methodologies for measuring marketing ROI. Most marketers (61%) indicated "some" cooperation between marketing and finance, while only 22% indicated full cooperation. In about one-half of the companies, respondents said that the marketing and finance departments don't speak with one voice or share common metrics.

If marketing is going to dodge the bullet and become a performance-driven organization, it needs new skills, tools, and perspectives, along with finance's help. It is time for marketing to overcome its adversarial relationship with finance and turn finance into an ally and at the same time turn marketing into a performance-driven operation within the organization.

Understanding the Finance Mindset

Basically, finance people are risk-averse. They need marketing to show them why what we want to do is the right thing to do. Marketers don't demonstrate their value by saying that marketing is strategic, but by being able to communicate how much money comes back and when. Finance is focused on revenue, expenses, profit, and shareholder value. For most companies, the old adage, "cash is king," still reigns. It's not that finance people aren't interested in the brand, but that they want to be able to link brand image and loyalty to financial business outcomes related to cash flow.

It isn't a coincidence that there is a strong correlation between cash flow and the responsibilities of marketing. Marketing is responsible for helping the organization acquire and keep profitable customers, which links us directly to cash flow. If we think in terms of customers, it becomes more apparent how marketing affects cash flow. First, each time marketing improves customer lifetime value it positively impacts cash flow. Marketing accelerates cash flow by enabling faster innovation and faster new product/service adoption rates. And it reduces the risk to business by lowering customer acquisition costs and customer churn. The more that marketing initiatives address customer lifetime value, improve the rate of product adoption, reduce customer churn, and lower acquisition costs, the better the company's cash flow.

When marketers talk in these terms, they are speaking the language of business and of the CFO. Marketers who understand the CFO's expectations and learn to speak that language are well on their way to creating an ally. If you don't understand the CFO's language, it's time to learn. There are four key words important to most every CFO:

- **Cash.**
- **EPS** (earnings per share).
- **Net contribution.**
- **Payback or payout** (the time frame within which an investment pays off).

When the leadership team asks about marketing ROI, they are really asking about payback. They want to understand how and when the investment marketing is making on behalf of the company will pay off. It's not that they don't want to give marketing the money it needs to do its job, but that they want to be able to analyze the tradeoffs between one investment and another. The company has only so many resources and can only make so many investments. Marketing programs are investments; some have a short-term payoff, some take longer to pay out. Marketers need to be able to communicate payback so the leadership team can determine which investment to make.

Behaving like a Strategic Business Unit Owner

Hopefully the CMO and the marketing team have come to understand that CFOs expect marketers to manage risk, to improve efficiency, and to be financially accountable. Really what they are asking is for marketing to act like a strategic business unit (SBU) owner. They want marketing organizations to know their numbers, have a plan, and demonstrate that they care about the company's success beyond their own particular piece of "turf."

If marketing accepts this role, then just like any other SBU owner it needs to demonstrate due diligence and accountability by focusing on incremental sales and gross margin contribution. SBU owners know their business and their key operational indicators. The CFO wants to know that we know our business. What kind of operational indicators communicate this to the CFO? The key operational indicators marketing should know at any moment include: the average purchase per customer, upgrade/cross-sell conversion ratio, customer lifetime value, average customer acquisition cost, average customer retention rate and cost, market share in each market segment and geographical division, and rate of new product acceptance. Jeremy Adamson, Global Controller for Consumer Products and Services at Symantec, once said that he expects any marketing executive to keep the following numbers in his/her head: "headcount, the revenue target for the quarter, the cost per revenue dollar, the cost per booking dollar, and your program-to-people ratio." If you don't know what numbers your CFO expects you to know at the drop of a hat, ask him or her.

If you are part of the marketing leadership team and aren't acting like an SBU owner, it's time to change. Only by recognizing that they are members of the business team will marketers be able to convert the CFO and finance into allies. In most companies, the SBU owner collaborates with finance to develop performance metrics for their business. Marketing needs to engage finance in the marketing planning and measurement process, just like any other SBU owner. If you aren't including finance in your plan development and review sessions, you are missing an important opportunity. Only by collaborating with finance can a marketing team make its journey to becoming a performance-driven organization a successful one.

Present a Business Case

When an SBU owner wants company money for an investment, they present a business case to the leadership team. Marketing needs to be able to articulate their business case in the same way as any other SBU owner. This is often where marketers fail. They don't appear to have done their homework. Any time they go to ask for money, even for the annual budget, they need to be able to justify the investment by addressing the following questions:

1. What is the *opportunity*?
2. Who is the *target market*?
3. What is the *strategic value* of the opportunity to the company?
4. What is the *potential return and profit*?
5. What is the *time to revenue*?
6. What is the *impact on revenue and sales capacity*?
7. What *other opportunities* will this impact?
8. What are the *risks*?
9. What are the *implications of losing this opportunity*?

Find Out What You Need to Shore up

Once marketers have learned the language of business and begun to act like an SBU, they may quickly realize that there are a few areas they need to shore up. We have found that marketing organizations typically face five challenges. The first is that the team's analytical and quantitative skills must be improved. The department needs to embrace the science side of marketing, rather than rely on its creative talents, which may mean re-training and personnel changes. The second challenge is that marketers must learn to understand and use statistics and data to drive decisions, rather than relying solely on experience, intuition, and opinion. Third, marketers may need to re-visit and reengineer the processes inside their organizations in order to achieve appropriate levels of granularity. Fourth, a marketing organization needs to ensure that it has a results-oriented and performance-driven culture. Finally, marketers need a set of measures and performance targets that are aligned with those of the company.

The CFO can actually help marketers with these challenges and transformations by helping them define realistic and appropriate marketing metrics. Once finance becomes engaged and starts thinking about marketing in a different way, marketing is one step closer to having finance as an ally. Once these challenges are met, marketers will find that their performance-driven team is integrated into the overall business.

Move the Needle

Making Finance an Ally

	Novice: • Learn the language of the CFO. • Demonstrate you know your numbers and have a plan. • Meet with the CFO to find out how many dollars in revenue each invested dollar is expected to generate.

	Intermediate:
	• Be able to account for the money you're getting now and the impact it is having.
	• Connect marketing programs to the customer buying process and demonstrate marketing's impact on customer acquisition, margin, and value.
	• Develop a set of operational metrics that prove you know your business (examples):
	  ◦ Average purchase per customer
	  ◦ Average Renewal rates
	  ◦ Upgrade / cross-sell conversions
	  ◦ Customer LTV (Lifetime Value)
	  ◦ Customer Acquisition Cost (CAC)
	  ◦ Customer Retention Cost (CRC)
	  ◦ Share in segment and Geography—velocity as well
	  ◦ New product acceptance

	Advanced: • Conduct a benchmark study that shows how you stack up against best-in-class performers. • Invest in your marketing operations function: It can be an effective liaise function and is a good grooming area to round out your high performers.

Notes

[1] Association of National Advertisers, and Marketing Management Analytics, Inc. (2007). *2007 Marketing Accountability Survey*, presented at the ANA Marketing Accountability Forum.

Sales and Marketing Alignment: Dancing to the Same Beat

According to the December 2007 study by the Aberdeen Group on Sales Effectiveness, "companies are under constant pressure to increase market share."[1] A common definition of market share is "the percentage of the total sales of a given type of product or service that are attributable to a given company."[2]

Increasing the total number of sales generally requires a company to acquire customers. Marketing is expected to increase the number of customers acquired faster and more cost effectively. Otherwise, companies would forgo marketing and just add more "feet on the street." That is, a company knows that in order to increase revenue by X%, the number of salespeople needs to increase. Similarly, there is a "right" amount of marketing investment required to produce a desired business outcome. Surely, with a marketing investment of $0, it would be impossible to achieve, say, $100M in sales. If a company wants to increase revenue it must recognize that marketing investment must grow along with sales investment.[3]

Marketing deploys a number of initiatives designed to increase preference, consideration, and purchase. By working together, sales and marketing can increase the organization's market share by improving the bid-to-win ratio and, thus, decreasing the cost of a qualified lead, two key performance criteria that distinguish what Aberdeen calls, Best-In-Class companies.

The dynamics of the 21st century are forcing businesses of all sizes and types to be able to react quickly and decisively to rapidly changing business and competitive conditions and changing customer demands. The more agile a company is, the faster it can respond to market dynamics and develop new products and processes, recognize new opportunities, and redeploy resources accordingly. The degree of a company's agility may be the difference between being a market leader instead of an also-ran. Agility requires proactive planning, business intelligence, alignment, and collaboration among all the key functions to make the right decisions and turn opportunities into competitive advantages. One of the key alignment issues facing many companies for years has been the alignment between marketing and sales.

Marketing and sales are really two sides of the same coin. They are both responsible for generating revenue for the company. Revenue is a result of a straightforward equation [Rev = (PipeOpp × Avg Deal × WinRate) / CycleTime) × Sellers]:

Opportunities in the pipeline multiplied by the average deal size multiplied by the win rate and then this product is divided by the sales cycle time. This result multiplied by all the sellers in your organization determines your revenue. Even a small increase in any of these variables can make a huge difference. The better marketing and sales are aligned, the more likely each of these factors can be improved, thereby increasing the company's revenue. Yet, the lack of alignment between marketing and sales inhibits many companies from achieving their revenue goals.

As a point of reference, some of the most recent research conducted by CSO Insights and IDC reveal four issues that are a result of this lack of alignment:

1. Longer sales cycles: Today's sales cycles are 25% longer than they were a year ago.
2. Missed quotas: Only about 43% of sales representatives (reps) made quota in 2006.
3. Productivity: Sales staff use up to 40% of their time each week developing materials to support their sales efforts.
4. Sales efficiency: Fewer than 25% of CMOs and 14% of senior sales executives are satisfied with their ability to optimize sales efficiency and effectiveness.

In a CMO Study conducted by Red Herring, 42% of the respondents listed marketing and sales alignment as one of the top crucial issues they need to address. It was third out of a list of ten issues.[4]

Déjà vu All over Again

This issue of marketing and sales alignment is not new. Most marketing and sales people have been in organizations where marketing has accused sales of not following up on leads and refusing to track leads through the sales cycle, and sales has accused marketing of not providing viable qualified leads. This misalignment is often attributed to a variety of factors, such as different goals, different performance targets and metrics, different timelines, and different psychologies. Market dynamics such as commoditization, Internet growth, mobility and virtualization, and changing business models only compound the problem.

Companies attempting to resolve the issue often approach the problem by trying to tighten the alignment of marketing activities within the sales cycle, improving coordination around lead generation, and increasing sales force participation in the marketing process. Sadly, these attempts often fail. Regardless of various approaches taken by companies to address this issue, the lack of alignment and collaboration between marketing and sales persists. Both organizations need to change for the company to succeed.

The first step to improve marketing and sales alignment and ultimately marketing and sales effectiveness is to shift from a transactional focus to a customer focus.

From Transactional to Customer Centricity

Achieving greater alignment begins with the marketing and the sales organizations deciding together which market segments offer the best opportunities and deserve the highest priorities. Today's buyers are more sophisticated and today's buying processes are more complex. The transactional approach of marketing generating qualified leads that sales then brings to a close is an outdated view. The transactional approach permits and even encourages marketing and sales to operate as independent, unrelated silos of business activities. This results in sales immersing itself in the latest training, engaging in calling on customers, and focusing on post-sale efforts; and marketing focusing on implementing various campaigns and coordinating a variety of tactics.

Customer Centricity takes a different view that requires a company to look at opportunity from the perspective of the customer: what they want from you, what they expect from you, and what they can count on from you. One way to develop customer centricity is to move away from a myopic selling perspective to a broader customer relationship lifecycle perspective. Taking a customer relationship lifecycle approach provides an avenue for alignment by focusing both the marketing and sales organizations on the same set of outcomes—creating, keeping, and increasing the value of customers.

The customer relationship lifecycle begins the moment a customer appears on the radar screen, moves into the lead-sales funnel, emerges as a customer, and engages in a variety of experiences that transform them into an advocate for your company. The customer relationship lifecycle provides insight into which customers provide the greatest lifetime value to your company.

The customer relationship lifecycle, in turn, enables the company to create a set of common metrics equally applicable to both sales and marketing organizations that will help ensure alignment. Customer relationship management metrics include buying-related metrics, such as recency, frequency, and quantity; cost-related metrics, such as gross amount of money spent on acquiring and retaining the customer through marketing dollars, resources spent generating each sale, and post sales service and support; and customer value-related metrics, such as the duration or longevity of that customer's relationship with your business, referral rate, and share of wallet. Establishing a common set of customer metrics facilitates alignment and collaboration and provides both organizations with a customer-oriented vocabulary and a set of priorities.

From Sales Funnel to Customer Buying Pipeline

We can transform a common tool, the sales funnel, used by many companies, as a way to improve alignment. The sales funnel is most often used by the sales organization to understand the flow of business opportunities. But the sales funnel has the opportunity to be so much more.

When developed properly, a sales funnel can serve as an important tool for improving marketing and sales alignment, thereby improving both organizations' performance. Funnel management provides insight into which sales and marketing processes are effective and increase deal flow, as well as insight into how efficiently customer opportunities are moving through the stages of opportunity development.

The first step in using the sales funnel for these purposes is to integrate it with the customer buying process. As a result, the sales funnel ceases to be merely a tool for the sales team. It has actually evolved into what should be called the buying pipeline. Why does this matter? A sales funnel suggests two things. First, the term suggests that this process is something owned by sales and not necessarily a shared responsibility across the organization. Yet, marketing plays a critical role in bringing potential buyers to the table. Marketing has the responsibility to identify, find, and secure profitable customers—that is, opportunities. Marketing also provides segmentation, customer targeting, positioning, product offers, and messaging to differentiate the company. Therefore, both the marketing and sales functions within the organization are essential to building the buying process. Second, it suggests a transactional approach rather than a customer-centric approach to the buying decision process.

By transforming the funnel into a pipeline you can begin the journey of marketing and sales alignment. Before developing your sales funnel, before defining your stages, before investing in a sales force automation tool or CRM system, map your ideal customer's buying process. We call this engineering the buying pipeline. This first step ensures that you understand why and how your customer makes a buying decision. It is possible that you will have to create more than one buying process map. Different segments may buy differently, and different products and services may have different purchasing processes.

Once you've mapped the process, the second step is to define each of the stages using incremental behavioral commitments. What is an incremental behavioral commitment? Let's use an everyday real-world example to illustrate the concept. When two people are both interested in finding a long-term relationship, they begin the courting process. Certain demonstrated behaviors along the way indicate whether the relationship is progressing toward the ultimate behavior of saying "I do." For example, showing up for the first date, the first kiss, introducing each other to best friends, to the family, saying "I love you," actually proposing, and so on are incremental behavioral commitments. This behavior demonstrates to both people

EXHIBIT 6.1 Buying Behavior Pipeline

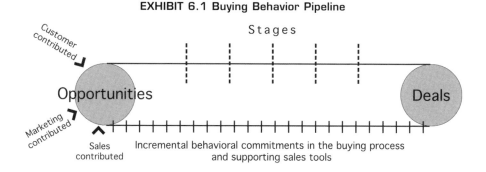

that the relationship is going from initial contact to ultimate deal. The question we have for you is whether you have a clear understanding of the specific incremental behaviors your customers actually demonstrate that show they are moving their commitment to the relationship forward. Until you do, you cannot create the buying pipeline, and until the pipeline is created, you will not have a funnel focused on customer opportunities.

Once you have the behaviors defined, you can take the third step and group the behaviors into stages. These stages will become the foundation for how you classify the status of each opportunity. Marketing can now develop tools appropriate for each stage, enabling the sales organization to appropriately engage with the prospective customer.

At the end of this journey you will have a pipeline that looks similar to Exhibit 6.1.

It's relatively easy to see how creating and properly using the buying pipeline serves as an excellent alignment and management tool. The idea behind pipeline management is that you can collect data throughout the process and continuously monitor multiple metrics, such as response-to-lead rate and response-to-sale rate. This data, over time, can then be used as a way to assess your marketing mix and evaluate the return on various marketing programs. The data can provide insight into which segments and mediums are performing as required and the types of prospects more likely to be qualified.

Pipeline management can also help identify where bottlenecks or gaps exist. For example, maybe there are too many contacts and the organization cannot process them quickly enough. Or there is a dearth of qualified leads, indicating that the sales team won't be able to produce the needed number of deals. We can also use the pipeline and associated processes to compare our program's performance to industry standards. Pipeline management allows you to calibrate your marketing organization and synchronize marketing and sales efforts. It also allows you to take a more metric-based approach to opportunity and customer development, enabling you to understand what is happening in the buying process and where to make adjustments. Pipeline management is really about managing opportunities. Opportunities represent customers, which takes us back to the need for transforming the traditional sales funnel into an integrated customer buying pipeline.

Abandoning the outdated view of the transactional approach to marketing—where marketing generates qualified leads that sales then brings to a close—in favor of a more customer-centric approach offers hope. It is the transactional approach that encourages marketing and sales to operate as independent silos, resulting in sales immersing itself in the latest training, engaging in calling on customers, and focusing on post-sale efforts, and marketing focusing on implementing various campaigns and coordinating a variety of tactics. Customer-centricity, on the other hand, requires a company to look at the world through the eyes of its customers—what they want, expect, and can count on from you.

The customer-centric approach enables you to move from looking at the world from a selling perspective to taking a customer relationship lifecycle perspective. Taking this approach provides an avenue for alignment by focusing both sales and marketing on the same set of outcomes—creating, keeping, and growing the value of customers. A customer-centric approach requires understanding the customer relationship lifecycle.

The customer relationship life cycle begins the moment customers appear on a company's radar screen, before they move into the lead-sales funnel, emerge as customers, and engage in a variety of experiences that result in them becoming advocates. Taking this life cycle as a perspective provides insight into which customers provide the greatest value to your company. As a result, the company can create a set of common metrics for sales and marketing that will help ensure alignment. These customer relationship management (CRM) metrics include buying-related metrics such as recency, frequency, and quantity; cost-related metrics such as gross amount of money spent on acquiring and retaining customers through marketing dollars, resources spent generating each sale, and post-sales service and support; and customer value-related metrics such as the duration or longevity of customers' relationship with your business, referral rate, and share of wallet. Establishing a common set of customer-centric metrics facilitates marketing-sales alignment and collaboration and provides both functions with a common customer-oriented vocabulary and set of priorities.

Once marketing and sales collaborate together to understand customers' needs and buying patterns, true alignment can occur.

Does Alignment Matter?

While no one can offer any guarantees, aligning marketing and sales makes good business sense and ultimately impacts the bottom line. A study conducted by Aberdeen on sales effectiveness with more than 200 respondents from the executive, sales, marketing, and IT management functions, found that companies that had strong marketing-sales collaboration achieve a higher sales effectiveness.[5] For many companies, this additional boon in sales more than justifies making the effort.

For example, ClearCube Technology sought out assistance in fostering sales and marketing alignment. Founded in 1997, ClearCube is the global market leader in PC Blade solutions. They deliver a managed desktop solution that provides Intel-based PC functionality to a user's desktop from a centralized environment.

In mid-2004 the company began to notice that sales growth was rapid, but that its ability to forecast sales accurately was not at an acceptable level. Jim Benard, Vice President of Worldwide Sales Operations, knew that accurate forecasts require that the sales process mirror the market's buying processes. He felt that an initiative was required to align the two. ClearCube was also implementing SalesForce.com, a hosted sales force automation tool, across its sales and marketing organizations and adding a significant number of new sales executives. Therefore, it was imperative that a more scientific and structured sales methodology with defined stages of the sales cycle was required in order to create a common language among the entire sales and marketing team and be quickly and effectively integrated into the new sales force automation toolset.

It Takes Work

ClearCube had previously implemented Siebel as its CRM application, but adaptation to the company's sales process was costly and never put into practice. The sales forecast process was cumbersome for the field sales organization and sales management. It also lacked a well-defined sales process: Pipeline management was inconsistent and lacked sufficient compliance from the sales team. The bottom line was that overall pipeline data were incomplete and inaccurate, and resulted in an unreliable sales forecast. The company realized it needed a new process. A buying pipeline development process was needed to improve marketing and sales alignment.

Three Steps to Better Alignment

The ClearCube case study illustrates three key steps any company can take to improve alignment.

Start with pipeline definition. In the first phase, a Pipeline Engineering Lab was conducted for more than 45 members of the ClearCube sales and marketing team. The Lab, a five-hour interactive work session, achieved the outcome of defining the buying pipeline stages and what is known as behavioral commitments for each stage of the buying process. Defining behavioral commitments was a fundamental difference in the new approach, which identifies observable behaviors performed by the prospective buyers and then maps the flow of these behaviors to the individual buyer's buying process. This creates pipeline stages from the buyers' perspective rather than determining them from the conditions set by the sales department. In this instance, the Lab participants defined eight stages and a large number of corresponding customer behaviors associated with each stage.

Refine the pipeline for automation. In the second phase, VEM worked with a hand-picked group of ClearCube marketing and sales managers to refine the pipeline further so that it could be implemented within the company's sales force automation application. The eight stages defined in the first phase were validated and named. The long list of behaviors from the Pipeline Lab was condensed so that each of the eight stages contained from 1 to 17 observable behaviors. In total, 74 distinct behaviors were listed. ClearCube's CRM administrator served as a key member of the team, ensuring that the final outcome could be implemented within SalesForce.com.

Then comes implementation. In the final phase, the new "buying pipeline" was incorporated into SalesForce.com in a manner that would be easy and fast for ClearCube's sales personnel to use. An FAQ (Frequently Asked Questions) document as well as an online Help document were prepared to facilitate training and adoption of the new pipeline process. In Benard's words, "The methodology succeeded in achieving critical 'buy-in' from sales executives, sales management, sales operations, top management, and marketing."

The benefits of alignment are clear. Three months after implementation, ClearCube's visibility into the flow of sales opportunities through the pipeline increased dramatically, bringing about greater alignment between sales and marketing. "We are now able to make forecasts [that] could be made with a much higher degree of reliability and accuracy than before," added Benard. "And sales and marketing share the same terminology when discussing the pipeline." It is also easier for marketing and sales to develop specific strategies and tactics because of the deeper insight into the customer behaviors that ClearCube is trying to affect.

While no one can offer any guarantees, aligning marketing and sales makes good business sense and ultimately improves the bottom line. A study conducted by Aberdeen on sales effectiveness with more than 200 executives from the executive, sales, marketing, and IT management functions found that companies that had strong collaboration between these two functions achieve higher sales effectiveness. By taking the two steps, From Transactional to Customer Centric and From Sales Funnel to Customer Buying Pipeline, your company can improve marketing and sales alignment in a relatively quick period of time and begin to reap the benefits of more revenue and profits. For many companies this additional boon in sales more than justifies making the effort.

Move the Needle

Align Sales and Marketing

	Novice: • Working with Sales, collaboratively define the customer buying process and create common definitions for each stage of the opportunity pipeline. • Develop sales enablement tools tied to specific stages within the customer buying process. • Create a centralized repository for all prospect and customer information. • Begin measuring qualified lead conversions and time-to-close.
	Intermediate: • Align marketing and sales compensation with common goals. • Formalize and automate all of the core processes needed to ensure alignment. • Implement and deploy a system that will automate the knowledge transfer between sales and marketing. • Establish a cross-functional team that is focused on improving alignment, collaboration and teamwork.
	Advanced: Develop a set of metrics that demonstrate marketing's contribution to the new opportunity acquisition process.

Notes

[1] Duhaime, G. (2007). "Sales and Marketing Alignment: United They Stand, Divided They Fall." *Aberdeen.com.* <http://www.aberdeen.com/summary/report /research_briefs/4691-RB-sales-n-mkt-alignment.asp>

[2] InvestorWords.com (2008). "Market Share (definition)." <http://www.investorwords.com /2989/market_share.html>

[3] Thanks to Stuart Itkin for his helpful comments on marketing spend. The author assumes responsibility for any divergence here from his intended meaning.

[4] Hanson, K. (2007). *Second Annual CMO Survey.* Presented to the Red Herring CMO Conference. <blog.marketo.com/blog/files/red_herring_second_annual_cmo_survey.pdf>

[5] Michiels, I. (2007). "The Convergence of Sales and Marketing Technologies." *Aberdeen.com.* <http://www.aberdeen.com/summary/report/benchmark/4177-RA-convergence-sales-technologies.asp>

Using a Quality Approach

Performance-driven marketing must have mechanisms in place to drive and track continuous improvement. One way to improve the quality of marketing's contribution to business in a manner that can be effectively measured and communicated is through the adoption of the Six Sigma approach. At the heart of Six Sigma is an organization's need to grow, improve its ability to meet customer requirements, and increase the opportunity to improve efficiency. The Six Sigma approach substitutes opinions and instinct in favor of data, analysis, and rigorous measurement. Every other organization in a company makes a contract with the leadership team about performance. If marketing wants to be perceived by the company as an essential function, it must do the same.

Growing Revenue

As someone who worked for Motorola from the early 1980s until the late 1990s, I had an opportunity to be a part of the Six Sigma Era. Even though Six Sigma as a measurement standard originated in the 1920s, Motorola is credited with applying the methodologies and coining the term. This approach differs from traditional quality improvement programs in its focus on input variables. While traditional process improvement methods depend upon measuring outputs and establishing control plans to shield customers from organizational defects, a Six Sigma program demands that problems be addressed at the input root-cause level, which eliminates the need for unnecessary inspection and the added costs for rework at the output stage.

The Six Sigma approach identifies and eliminates defects with a structured, data-driven, problem-solving method of using rigorous data-gathering and statistical analysis. Its statistical representation describes quantitatively how a process is performing. To achieve Six Sigma, a process must not produce more than 3.4 defects per million opportunities. The philosophy here is that if you can reduce process variation, you can improve organizational effectiveness and efficiency.

According to General Electric—an early adopter of the program—Six Sigma is a "highly disciplined process that helps us focus on developing and delivering near-perfect products and services" and "systematically figure out how to . . . get as close to 'zero defects' as possible."[1] Originally used to improve engineering and manufacturing, the Six Sigma approach has expanded to include all aspects of organizational performance.

Among the top 100 Fortune 500 companies, over half of them use Six Sigma methodology in some part of their business.[2] Seventy of the top 100 companies have been in the top 100 for five or more years, and 44 of these 70 companies (63%) implement Six Sigma to some degree. These 44 Six Sigma users report on average 49% higher profits (compounded annually) and 2% higher compounded annual growth revenue (CAGR) than their peers.

In short, Six Sigma enables companies to improve marketing's strategic, tactical, and operational processes as a way to enhance the top line to drive revenue. The Six Sigma philosophy emphasizes a customer-centric approach by focusing the organization on satisfying customer requirements. It is this customer-centric philosophy that provides common ground between marketing and Six Sigma.

By applying this approach, marketing can develop lean, efficient workflows, identify leading indicators of growth, and become proactive about performance improvement. Measurement of performance is one of the five fundamental phases in the Six Sigma methodology. Once you begin measuring marketing performance, you can begin to make modifications and improvements. A key part of the Six Sigma process is mapping, which helps people identify areas for efficiency improvement and cost reductions.

We can illustrate the Six Sigma mapping process by applying it to customer experience mapping. As we've noted several times throughout this book, the purpose of business is to find, keep, and grow the value of customers. A customer's experience impacts his/her desire to continue to do business with a company. Therefore, as business and marketing professionals, we should know whether we are delivering a good experience and be able to use customer experience metrics to identify where to improve, so this is an ideal example for illustrating how to apply Six Sigma to marketing.

We all know the old adage, "If you can't measure it, you can't manage it." Most organizations tend to measure customer experience by measuring satisfaction. While degree of satisfaction is an important part the customer experience, because of its impact, customer experience merits its own independent measurement.

To measure the customer experience, you need to establish and follow the disciplined process associated with Six Sigma as a way to reveal what truly matters to your customers. The purpose of the process is to help determine a set of internal metrics that define a quality customer experience, provide a clear view into the customer interactions and contact points that are critical to a quality experience, identify the relative importance customers place on the interactions with your company, clarify your customers' expectations, and ultimately create a methodology for continuous improvement.

The customer experience mapping process entails five steps:

1. Define the customer experience.
2. Establish experience expectations, priorities, and performance perceptions.
3. Map the customer experience against these priorities and performance perceptions.

4. Identify and measure opportunities for improvement.
5. Create a customer experience scorecard.

Defining the customer experience is the first step in the process. To complete this step, identify every part of the customer experience and then organize them into the common experience in order to construct, diagram, and draw the process. This process should include steps, contact points, and interactions for relationship initiation, provider evaluation, account creation, order placements, product receipt and usage, problem resolution, payment, and customer relationship management.

Below is an abbreviated example of a first-time customer experience from initial contact through the purchase and post-purchase process. Once you've outlined the process, you will need to make sure the perception of this process and the definitions are consistent throughout your organization. You may need to engage customers in this step in order to capture their point of view. After all, you are mapping the customers' experiences and their perceptions, not your internal perspective. It may be helpful to create the process from the inside out and then again with input from the customer (from the outside in) as a way to expose any perceptual gaps.

After you validate the flow, label each contact point/interaction with a distinct and unique name or code. You will need this information when you create the map.

To complete the customer experience, you may need to survey your customers, preferably those with the most recent experience (so you can capture memories as fresh as possible) and those who represent your most typical customers. The best way to capture their input is by conducting in-depth interviews. During this step you will also want to capture the expectations, importance, and perception of your company's performance at each contact point. We strongly advise that you provide customer participants with an honorarium and use a third party for this process so customers will be candid and forthcoming. It is very important to never presume for the customer. You want the questions to be as general and as neutral as possible. Using the example in Exhibit 7.1, some possible survey questions might include:

- When you first came to the XYZ web site, can you describe your initial reaction?
- When you attended the industry conference, can you describe how you were greeted?
- When you registered for the webinar, can you describe what happened? How did this meet with your expectation?

The purpose of this step is to pare down the customer experience to a short list of the most critical interactions and product and service requirements. Upon completion of this step, you will have some interesting insights, but you will need to complete the rest of the steps to create metrics and a basis for action.

EXHIBIT 7.1 The Customer Experience Mapping Process

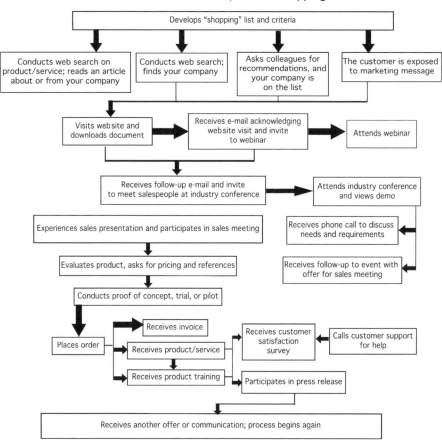

Once you have the map, create a scoring methodology for importance and experience. For example, you might use 1-10 rating for importance, with 10 being critical to retention and loyalty and a 1-10 rating on performance, with 10 being an experience far exceeding expectation. You will combine all the scores from customers and all the internal scores and indicate them on the map. Upon completion of this step you will be able to determine where you are doing well and where there are opportunities for improvement.

Exhibit 7.2 shows a common map including the key elements. It is useful to weight each contact point to reflect the relative importance of that interaction to the customers.

You can then plot a graph of the experience map (Exhibit 7.3) and compare the experience between contact points as well as compare the perceptions of performance between customers and internal staff.

Now that you have information about what your customers care about and you

EXHIBIT 7.2 Typical Criteria for a Customer Experience Map

	Contact Point Number	Contact Point Number	Contact Point Number	Contact Point Number	Contact Point Number	Contact Point Number	Contact Point Number	Contact Point Number
Combined Customer Importance Score								
Combined Customer Experience Score								
Total Weighted Score for Customers								
Combined Internal Importance Score								
Combined Internal Performance Score								
Total Weighted Score for Internal								

EXHIBIT 7.3 Graph Plotting a Customer Experience Map

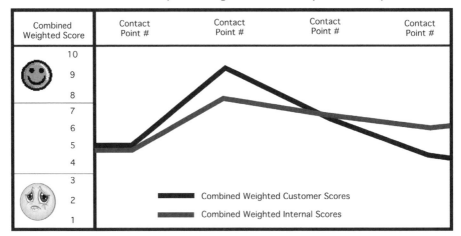

have created a combined score, you can begin to develop a scorecard. To create the scorecard you will first need to establish some performance targets against which you will measure your progress and decide which contact points and interactions are the most critical for creating a competitive advantage and building loyalty. The scorecard will help you identify the internal metrics that link directly to the customer's experience.

Mapping the customer experience is an important business process for all organizations. Creating a customer experience map compels a company to take a customer-centric view.

The customer experience map provides a good example of how the Six Sigma mapping process can be a key part of a performance-driven marketing organization. As businesses renew their focus on the customer and as the marketing organization faces more pressure to improve efficiency and reduce costs, the Six Sigma methodology provides a well-defined approach. Six Sigma provides both a methodology for process improvement and a way to prove its value. Every marketing process can be mapped and process improvement made. These additions are above and beyond the traditional Six Sigma approach to cost reduction.

The Methodologies of Six Sigma

Six Sigma has two methodologies: DMAIC and DMADV (Exhibit 7.4). DMAIC is used to improve existing business processes, and DMADV is used to create new process or product designs that result in more predictable, mature, and defect-free performance. Each methodology includes five steps that we will mention here. However, for the purpose of this chapter we will focus on the DMAIC process.

The purpose of these two methodologies is to create a data-driven, systematic approach to solving business problems that will have a positive impact on cus-

EXHIBIT 7.4 DMAIC and DMADV

D	**Define** roles, goals, and deliverables consistent with customer demands and the organization's strategy
M	**Measure** current performance and processes, and collect relevant data for future comparison and improvement
A	**Analyze** the relationship and causal factors
I	**Improve** the process to eliminate defects
C	**Control and correct** any variances before they result in defects, thereby improving performance
D	**Define** the goals of the design activity
M	**Measure** and identify the critical quality, product/process capabilities
A	**Analyze** to develop and design alternatives to demonstrate the best design
D	**Design** the process
V	**Verify** the design

tomers. Let's consider how we can apply the five-step DMAIC process to marketing in order to grow revenue:

1. **Define:** The role of marketing is to create predictable streams of revenue growth by enabling the organization to identify profitably and secure new customers, and to keep and grow the value of these customers. Therefore, a key ingredient in this step is for marketing to establish goals and deliverables designed to achieve these outcomes. This will require most organizations to broaden the role of marketing beyond sales support and/or marketing communications into a more strategic role. As a result, the various marketing functions will need to be integrated to create a comprehensive workflow process. This integrated workflow process will then need to be mapped. Once these elements are completed, new metrics that tie marketing to business outcomes must be defined and standardized across the marketing organization for the purposes of providing insight into performance and facilitating strategic decisions. Typically, it will become apparent that new analytical and process-oriented skills will be needed among the marketing personnel.

2. **Measure:** Measurement is a prerequisite for determining marketing ROI (return on investment). There is no escaping the fact that to be successful in measurement, marketing needs data. Without quality data, performance

cannot be measured and improvements cannot be made. Marketing needs to have access to data about its efforts and expenditures. It will need to have a collaborative relationship with finance, sales, and customer service because these groups are often the keepers of critical data related to performance and outcomes. Marketing will also need to deploy tools and systems for capturing and monitoring data. During this step the team will need to make key decisions related to the data including: how well it will be managed, how well it will be shared, and what processes will be used for evaluation.

The first step in measuring and improving performance is to determine what data exist, where those data are, what data are needed, and how to obtain the data. Customer purchase activity, marketing program results and conversion rates, actual costs for programs and people, lead quality data and lead cost, win/loss ratios, and defections that occur in the buying process are examples of some of the data that will be needed. Once the metrics are defined, the team should use the data to establish a baseline of past expense and performance.

Measurement suggests that current and future performance are being compared to past performance. Being able to establish a benchmark using past data is an important step that eludes most marketing organizations because of the lack of quality data. It may take considerable effort to establish the initial data points, but this step is essential to the process.

The metrics should be defined not just in terms of cost, but in terms of how these investments contributed to the company's ability to achieve its goals and generate profit. The marketing metrics are contingent upon knowing business outcomes. It is imperative that business outcomes be clarified and specified before the marketing metrics are established. For example, business outcomes may be related to the specific number of customers to be acquired and at what cost, the specific rate of customer acquisition, the specific lifetime value of a customer, customer loyalty, and specifically how quickly customers adopt new products. By knowing business outcomes, marketing knows what objectives it needs to achieve and within what parameters. Marketing can now establish metrics and performance targets and processes, and can measure its performance. Tying marketing metrics to business outcomes forces marketing to transform from a transactional function to a strategic contributor.

3. **Analyze:** Simply measuring performance will not make it improve. There is an important role for analysis and analytics in marketing. Analytics is the method of logical analysis. Analysis generally entails examining separate elements and understanding the relationship among the elements. Analysis using quality data and analytics are crucial to performance-driven marketing organizations. By analyzing performance and using analytics marketing organizations can begin to pinpoint sales drivers, forecast sales from future

marketing activities, evaluate why something differed from the expected results, and identify the most profitable allocation of marketing resources. Today's environment is forcing organizations frequently to adjust their strategies, processes and technologies used to identify, acquire and retain profitable customers. Performance improvement related to these efforts are derived from insights gleaned from data analysis. By analyzing the data and understanding what they mean, marketing can determine the degree of impact it is having on the organization, and redesign processes that will improve performance.

Creating a dashboard of key business initiatives can help process the data and make it easier to visualize both the impact of marketing and opportunities for improvement. Analyzing marketing performance and processes has impact beyond the marketing organization. The analysis may yield information that will impact sales, product development, customer service, accounting, and IT. Marketing exists as a component within the overall company organizational system, and changes to this part of the system can serve as a catalyst for changes in another part of the business. Analysis leads right into the next step, improvement.

4. **Improve:** The main purpose of applying Six Sigma to marketing is to determine how to improve performance and processes. Data analysis should result in valuable insights that generate possibilities for improvement. These possibilities for improvement can include enhancements in tools, systems, processes, and skills. A performance-driven marketing organization welcomes opportunities for improvement. Even though change is disruptive, developing new ways to approach the market enables the marketing organization to play a more strategic role in the business.

   As you have probably surmised, you need to repeat the Measure-Analyze-Improve steps until the optimal processes are defined and the optimal performance is achieved. These repeated steps enable continuous improvement.

5. **Control and Correct:** Because marketing prides itself on its creativity, it has often sacrificed control. But the time has come for marketing to document its processes and best practices, and to apply these consistently. The lack of standards control will result in less-than optimal marketing execution. An emerging role, marking operations, provides the organization with a function and with people responsible for ensuring that the knowledge gained through process improvement is documented and implemented. Regardless of whether your company establishes this role, it is imperative that the team establish and document the processes implemented in the previous steps and ensure people adhere to them. Even if the organization establishes this role, everyone on the team needs to be formally trained in the processes and performance metrics. The entire team must understand how the processes enable marketing to demonstrate its value and improve its performance.

Applying Six Sigma to marketing will increase marketing's ability to deliver on market requirements, improve the efficiency and effectiveness of the marketing planning process, successfully manage marketing operations, provide transparency into marketing processes, and improve the collaboration between marketing and other groups within the business. Marketing has a strategic role in growing revenue. For the marketing team to provide valuable contributions to business profitability, they must assume a broader set of responsibilities within the company. One proven method of integrating marketing operations within the overall business process is through Six Sigma and its DMAIC methodology. Six Sigma enables companies to improve marketing's strategic, tactical and operational processes as a way to enhance the top line to drive revenue and experience higher profits and growth.

Move the Needle

Applying Six Sigma to Marketing

	Novice: • Gather the marketing team and discuss the DMAIC methodology. • Define your goals and develop an action plan within the next 30–60 days to measure current performance in achieving these goals.
	Intermediate: • Analyze your marketing organization's current performance in achieving its goals for business. • Use the mapping process to identify opportunities to reduce cost, increase efficiency and improve performance. • Develop an action plan within the next 30-60 days based on your findings.
	Advanced: • Establish a marketing operations role in your organization responsible for controlling and reporting marketing performance. If you cannot establish such a role explicitly, make sure the members of your team can accountably implement and track performance. • Lead the initiative to engage customers in dialogue designed to identify their requirements, how well your organization is meeting these, and where there are opportunities for improvement.

Notes

[1] General Electric (2008). "What is Six Sigma? The Roadmap to Customer Impact," *GE.com.* <http://www.ge.com/sixsigma/SixSigma.pdf>

[2] Creveling, C., L. Hambleton, and B. McCarthy (2006). *Six Sigma for Marketing Processes: An Overview for Marketing Executives, Leaders, and Managers.* New York: Prentice Hall.

Marketing Operations: The Science Side of Marketing

The world's markets are becoming more and more efficient as the demand to drive inefficiency out of companies continues to expand. These demands for better efficiency are dramatically impacting the marketing function. As complexity increases and rates of change continue to accelerate, marketing departments are becoming the center of corporate attention. As a result, marketing organizations face both external challenges from competition and internal challenges related to people, processes, systems, and tools. In order to rise to these challenges, marketing is undergoing a transformation that will enable it to improve its operational and business performance. The stronger the link between what marketers envision in their strategies and what they execute in the marketplace, the more they can ensure that marketing is providing value. There has been movement toward creating a marketing operations role to drive home the connection between marketing strategy, execution, and actual results in performance-driven marketing.

IDC first identified the rise of the marketing operations (MO) function early in 2005 and provided a detailed analysis and framework for the staffing requirements and responsibilities as industry guidance for this role's contribution to the marketing organization. At that time, marketing operations served to identify and drive real process change. It was up to the marketing operation function to instill change in the organizational processes of marketing and to act as an agent of change to improve marketing's credibility in the organization from a fiscal management perspective.

IDC indicated that the ability to collaborate with sales, finance, and IT to establish the foundation for marketing managerial accounting was key to marketing operations success. In a few short years, marketing operations had gained a key role within the marketing organization.

In 2007, Marketing Operations Partners conducted a benchmarking study, "Journey to Marketing Operations Maturity," to understand the discipline of Marketing Operations and how well it is currently being deployed in companies. Best-in-class marketing operations develop a performance measurement process that cascades from corporate objectives to marketing objectives to marketing programs. The study found that the top three priorities for MO are the measurement of marketing ROI and demonstration of value, balancing marketing strategy with tactics, and tying marketing success to the goals of other groups.

What exactly is a Marketing Operations and what does it include? Marketing Operations Partners defines it as "a thorough, end-to-end operational discipline that leverages processes, technology, guidance, and metrics to run the Marketing function."[1] The benchmarking study found that marketing operations in best practice firms include measurement, planning, process improvements, marketing IT, budget/financial management, marketing intelligence, sales, and other stakeholder alignment within the function. Essentially, marketing operations builds a foundation for excellence by reinforcing marketing strategy with metrics, process, infrastructure, and best practices.

The Need for MO

The marketing operations function has emerged as a result of the need for a more transparent, efficient, and accountable view of marketing. And this role has been expanding over recent years throughout the business world. The purpose of marketing operations is to increase both marketing efficiency and to build a foundation for excellence by reinforcing marketing with processes, technology, metrics, and best practices. Marketing operations enables an organization to run the marketing function as a fully accountable business. It is about performance, financial management, strategic planning, marketing resources, skills assessment, and management. A performance-driven organization views operations as an enabler for success. So it stands to reason that a performance-driven marketing organization should establish a marketing operations function.

Establishing marketing operations capabilities does not come without challenges. For many organizations it is a new discipline and a new function. It is interesting that the top priorities for most marketing operations are also its biggest challenges. According to the Marketing Operations Partners study, marketing operations face a number of common challenges, including measuring marketing ROI and demonstrating value; achieving optimal balance between strategy and tactics; tying common goals for marketing success to other groups; justifying marketing's role and contribution to the C-suite; and making sure the marketing process enables internal efficiencies and effectiveness.[2]

Marketing's Primary Responsibilities

This chapter outlines some of marketing operations' primary responsibilities. As the role has evolved it has come to encompass the following five main areas:

1. Defining and managing systems and tools.
2. Developing and implementing metrics, infrastructure, and business processes.

3. Establishing and communicating best practices.
4. Managing the overall marketing budget and budgeting process.
5. Identifying and deploying technology to support performance measurement and reporting.

Let's explore each of these areas and try to understand each responsibility's function and importance.

Process: The Foundation for Alignment

One of the chief complaints about marketing is that it lacks alignment with sales, finance, and R&D. Therefore, it is essential for marketing to define and establish processes that facilitate alignment with these areas. The role of marketing operations is to develop and manage an integrated process of systems and tools that includes setting performance goals, modeling, planning, and reporting. A marketing operations function should ensure that the right processes are in place to support performance management and measurement.

In addition, marketing operations personnel should be able to define and secure the systems and tools needed to enable marketing operations. These tools and processes will analyze and identify overlaps, gaps, bottlenecks, and redundancies in order to suggest process improvements. These improvements will in turn support marketing's ability to help the organization achieve its goals and objectives. It also falls to marketing operations to develop the infrastructure and marketing systems that will promote the effective use of technology throughout the marketing organization. Marketing operations staff must define, document, and standardize core marketing processes and collaborate with finance, sales, and R&D to ensure organizational alignment around the processes and performance targets.

The Linkage of Marketing Dashboards and Marketing Operations

Today there is really no shortage of data. The gap is in our ability to use these data to gain a sustained competitive advantage and to drive specific business outcomes. To be successful, marketing needs both accurate current and historical data and the ability to recognize patterns that connect seemingly unrelated data points. One of our key challenges in marketing is to develop a baseline for metrics that helps us better evaluate performance and drive marketing decisions. Marketers need to understand measurement and create a metrics framework that links marketing to a bigger business objective. Marketing measurement is about more than just the finances and payback; it is about creating value and growth. Therefore, it is critical to have a function that helps define the measurement system, process, and performance targets. Marketing operations fulfills this role while creating access to the data needed to create useful dashboards.

Because marketing operations creates a repository of information and facilitates implementation of the systems, support, and infrastructure, it provides a much-needed focal point for performance management. The difference between success and failure is really not the dashboard or even the information reflected in the dashboard but, rather, what we do with the information and how we use it to make decisions. This is the point behind marketing metrics and marketing performance management: to use metrics to fine-tune investments, manage the marketing mix, and provide guidance and governance for decision-making.

Marketing metrics should reflect the company's priorities and objectives, and the dashboards created by marketing operations should guide effective and timely decision-making. Dashboards synthesize our knowledge and highlight gaps. They visually align tactics, strategies, and objectives with business outcomes, serving as a visual representation of and guide for performance.

Setting Realistic Expectations for Performance and Accountability

To take a leadership role in an organization marketing needs a set of core marketing and change management processes and practices to help to ensure that marketing personnel know how best to use the processes, systems, and metrics that are developed. Marketing operations needs to be the keeper of techniques, methods, activities, and processes that are effective in delivering a particularly superior outcome or result. As the keeper, marketing operations is responsible for the knowledge transfer, skills development, and benchmarking needed to sustain success. Marketing's best practices need to be able to span activities and tactical execution along with marketing campaign management, marketing and sales effectiveness tools, Internet and direct marketing, and market and customer research, as well as enterprise marketing management, brand and marketing resource management, digital asset management, and marketing process management.

The trend of increasing marketing accountability shows no sign of abating. The need to be able to tie marketing activities and investments to results will continue. As a result there will be continued pressure on marketing executives and professionals to demonstrate an understanding of how they are driving their company's brand value, incremental revenue, and customer equity. As marketers, we need to focus on developing and enhancing the science side of our skill set and on leveraging marketing operations either as a function and/or a discipline to create a culture based more on facts than intuition. Even with a marketing operations function in place, a marketing organization cannot succeed without embracing a performance-driven, accountable culture. Such a culture requires that knowledge be accessible to every one on the team so that each person has a view into the entire scope of work and visibility into the processes, budget, execution, metrics, and reporting required. Such a culture has an unwavering belief that performance starts with accountability. Marketers must never lose sight of the need to be both efficient and effective, and must realize that metrics and measurement practices are essential not only to tracking performance but also as the means to improve results.

It has been proven that marketing operations is a critical driver of marketing performance management and creating a performance-driven organization. How does one go about establishing a high performance marketing operations organization? The first step is to develop a strategy roadmap that addresses the processes, data, resources, talent/skills, systems, and metrics. A roadmap describes a future environment, objectives to be achieved within that environment, and plans for how those objectives will be achieved over time. The purpose of this roadmap is to communicate the overall direction, priorities, and execution strategy for a marketing operations function.

In keeping with the view that marketing must connect to business outcomes, the marketing operations strategy and roadmap must focus the initiative on how the strategy and its implementation will enable the organization to achieve these outcomes. The process we recommend is designed to develop a marketing operations roadmap that focuses on those areas that will have the maximum value and contribution to the business.

Our experience suggests that there are three key steps for creating the marketing operations strategy roadmap: strategy development, assessment, and development and delivery of a project-ready roadmap:

- Strategy Development: To define the vision and strategy, you must first understand what the organization believes is the role of marketing and the role of marketing operations and planning in achieving the organization's business outcomes. Strategy development requires understanding the strategic priorities the company has set for marketing and how marketing operations is expected to help achieve organizational goals. We typically recommend interviewing key stakeholders to gain this insight.
- Assessment: It is difficult to determine where you are going to go and how you are going to get there if you do not know where you are and the current capabilities. Once the information from the first step is completed, the next step is to assess the current marketing operations capabilities and performance and to compare this against other marketing operations practitioners. In this phase, existing processes, data, metrics, analytics, plans and strategies and marketing operations best practices are reviewed in preparation for the roadmap development meeting discussed. This step provides insight into gaps and areas of strength and opportunity for use in the roadmap development.
- Roadmap Development: Once the strategy is clarified and the

assessment is completed, a specific action plan/road map can be developed to close gaps and leverage opportunities. To begin the road map development process, VEM recommends a cross-functional team participate in an offsite one-day strategy session. The purpose of the session is to identify requirements and elements of the execution plan to build operational capabilities.

Measuring marketing performance is a leadership trait of high-performance marketing organizations. To become a performance-driven organization, marketing operations is critical because only with efficient and precise operations can the business strategies be supported.

Move the Needle

Marketing Operations

	Novice: • Gain executive support and establish initial role and responsibilities. • Define goals and charter for the organization. • Establish initial processes for measuring and reporting performance.
	Intermediate: • Assess the marketing operations function and identify gaps and strengths. • Drive more effective strategic planning, investment decisions, and budgeting processes. • Pave the way for marketing performance measurement processes. • Create and implement a strategy roadmap.
	Advanced: • Identify and deploy the required infrastructure to maintain the consistent implementation of processes. • Build the skills needed to sustain a performance-driven marketing organization. (See Chapter 14 on Skills and Training for specific skill-building recommendations.)

Notes

[1] Marketing Operations Partners (2006). "What Is Marketing Operations?" *Mopartners.com.* <http://www.mopartners.com/aboutus/whatis.php>
[2] Ibid.

SECTION III

From Ideas to Practice

The previous sections discussed the need for and factors that enable marketing to become a performance-driven organization. This section turns to how marketers can implement the recommended changes and move the needle for the business. It is hard to know where you need to go and how to get there if you don't know where you are and what capabilities and resources you have at hand and those you need to acquire. Several tools are introduced to help you determine where you are. These include the metrics continuum, mapping, and an audit.

The metrics continuum helps organizations begin to understand the role of various metrics and provides a vehicle for how to categorize what is measured. For marketing to meet the expectations of the C-suite it must evolve its measurement practices in order to be able to demonstrate and predict its financial impact on the bottom line.

A mapping process that enables marketing to ensure alignment with the business and begins to define the appropriate metrics is introduced in this section.

Understanding where your marketing organization is in terms of measuring performance doesn't come from abstract contemplation, but from the concrete evaluation that is a result of auditing. The audit process helps identify a trajectory that can be further developed through mapping and the development of a marketing dashboard and specification. It also helps evaluate what systems, tools, processes and skills are required to create a more performance-driven organization.

Contributing authors have added a perspective to this section by providing insight into how systems, tools, and skills development are key enablers that truly make a difference. The systems, tools and training are essential ingredients every marketing organization needs in order to move the needle and communicate marketing's impact across the business.

The Metrics Continuum: A Framework

Whether it's coming from the C-suite or the marketing organization, the drive for measuring marketing performance is gaining momentum. In order for a marketing organization to become performance driven, there must be an understanding of how to measure performance beyond the tracking of particular marketing activities. This chapter presents a marketing metrics continuum and suggestions for applying different metrics in order to improve marketing performance and move the needle for business.

Déjà vu—Again

The issue of measuring marketing is not a new one. We've already identified numerous studies from as early as the 2000 study conducted by the Advertising Research Foundation that revealed "enhanced return on marketing investment" as one of the top priorities CEOs set for their marketing and research functions. In a recent survey of 825 executives and professionals conducted by the CMO Council, a majority of respondents identified the measurement of marketing performance as a key challenge for 2008.[1] VisionEdge Marketing's own research over the years has found that fewer than 9% of marketing professionals and executives are satisfied with how well their organizations are tracking performance, and a majority list marketing performance measurement as one of their top three priorities for 2008. While the research shows that there's been a great deal of discussion about measuring performance as well as some improvement, progress has still been slower than desired.

Why can't we do it? A 2006 study by Deloitte & Touche found that the lack of well-defined measurement capabilities and the lack of internal coordination and clearly defined accountabilities served as two of the biggest challenges executives face when it comes to improving measuring marketing effectiveness.[2]

Measurement is at the center of improvement. It provides timely feedback, enables corrective action, provides focus, and gives the organization the ability to design, map, and monitor processes, and adopt best practices. Measuring marketing performance begins with metrics. Metrics drive and enable the organization to see what is working, adjust as needed, and bridge gaps. Today's budget- and resource-

EXHIBIT 9.1 Biggest Marketing Challenges Source: Deloitte & Touche.

What have been your biggest challenges in improving measuring marketing effectiveness? (n=460)

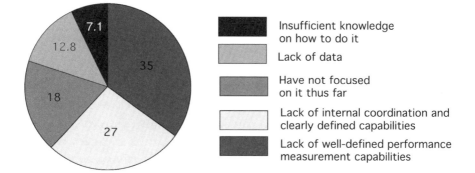

Insufficient knowledge on how to do it

Lack of data

Have not focused on it thus far

Lack of internal coordination and clearly defined capabilities

Lack of well-defined performance measurement capabilities

constrained environment mandates that the organization be able to discern which marketing efforts make a difference.

Measurement Frameworks

There are many measurement frameworks available. The challenge for marketing is what to measure. In today's environment we can easily become lost in a sea of metrics. Marketing professionals today have a host of metrics to choose from—from business acquisitions/demand generation metrics such as market share gains, category growth, customer acquisition, brand awareness and preference to product innovation/acceptance metrics such as market adoption rates, new products as a percentage of revenue, time-to-revenue, user attachment & affinity, share of wallet, loyalty and referral rates to corporate value metrics, such as growth in brand value and financial equity, customer franchise value, price premium, retention of customers and employees, customer engagement, and brand championship to corporate vision and leadership metrics such as share of voice, share of distribution, retention & message relevance and tonality of coverage. I recall one vice president of marketing who proudly claimed he tracked 200 marketing metrics each month, while a recent book has identified more than 50 metrics every executive should master.[3]

We have found that too many measures can actually impede progress and that the wrong metrics may make things worse. The goal of metrics is to help us work smarter and empower people to make decisions and take action. We should select metrics that can provide a current picture (for example, rate of customer acquisition, product margins, and close rate) and indicate future performance (for example, share of preference, share of wallet, and net advocacy).

Instead, it helps to think of metrics along a continuum (Exhibit 9.2).

The continuum of marketing metrics enables marketing organizations to or-

EXHIBIT 9.2 The Metrics Continuum

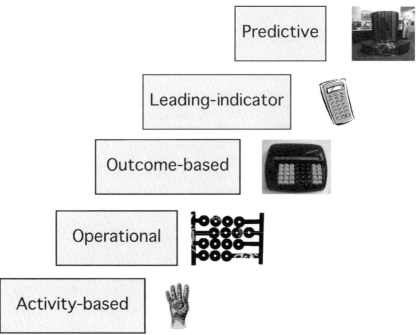

ganize their metrics from tactical to strategic. Performance-driven organizations have metrics all along the continuum. What differentiates these organizations is that they have moved beyond merely measuring their activities and have evolved their measurement frameworks to incorporate metrics from further along in the continuum. In what follows we discuss the different metrics along the continuum and how marketing organizations can use the continuum as a framework for marketing performance measurement.

In the Beginning, There was Counting

As the creative side of marketing began to give way to the analytical data-driven side, counting took center stage. Marketers looked for various things to count and various numbers to report. *Activity-based metrics*, which represent marketing's first foray into the world of measurement, refer to things like press hits, click-through rates, CPMs (cost-per-thousand), and so on (Exhibit 9.3). Most marketing plans today consist of activity lists, such as the numbers of ads to run, trade shows to attend, the number of direct marketing campaigns, new product brochures to produce, research studies to conduct, and so on. Marketing organizations then report on the results of these activities, such as the number of responses to the ad, how many people attended the event, the number of people who downloaded the new brochure. While

EXHIBIT 9.3 Activity-Based Metrics

	Activity	Last Year's Results	Next Year's Target
Activity-Based Metrics: Counting	Aided Brand Awareness	50%	>50%
	Leads/Rep	150	1,200
	References/Industry	15	20
	Analyst Wins	2	3
	Press Hits	200	300
	Product Awards	1	3

marketing must indeed keep track of its activities and the results, activity-based metrics give us little or no information on the impact of these activities on the business. The company cannot make any key business decisions or determine whether their strategies are working. Nor can marketers communicate the value of their contribution to the company.

Metrics that typically track the number of occurrences or people are generally in this category. Even if this is where you are, you should at least establish performance targets against which to measure.

The Value of Metrics

Then there came value and accountability, the two primary operative words in business. A number of marketing organizations have developed metrics for the next point on the continuum—*operational metrics*. These metrics begin to enable marketing to manage the marketing function as a business. Companies who have reached this point on the continuum often need additional skills within the organization and hire people such marketing operations directors or the marketing finance directors. Operational metrics are designed to improve organizational efficiency and ROI. Program-to-people ratios, marketing spend/person, marketing spend/revenue, awareness-to-demand ratios, the cost/lead, the cost/sale, and conversation rates embody marketing's increasing proficiency in numbers and its improved alignment with sales. These operational metrics make the connection between marketing, "programs," and business outputs stronger. Operational metrics take a marketing organization one step forward. There is just one small hiccup: Operational metrics primarily provide the organization with a way to rationalize marketing investments, but not with a way that relates marketing back to strategy and business performance.

Businesses are about securing revenue-producing customers, keeping these customers, and growing the amount of profitable revenue derived from the customer franchise. Yet most operational metrics do not account for these outcomes. A marketing metrics framework must demonstrate how marketing enables the organization to realize these outcomes. If marketing can't move beyond using activity-based and operational metrics alone, the discipline of marketing faces becoming merely sales support and loses its ability to influence organizational strategy.

Here's an example. A well-established public applications software company with thousands of customers has a very creative and responsive marketing organization. Every time a business unit brings a new product to market or has an idea for a marketing program, they show up at the marketing organization's door with a list of items and activities they want. When marketing is unable to link many of its activities either to motivating customers to buy more product or to make referrals—the two key measures the C-suite uses to define success—marketing loses leverage. Further, marketing cannot provide strategic advice as to which activities and/or programs matter. Until marketing determines which efforts are directly linked to business outcomes, it will continue to be bombarded with requests from the business units and sales that cannot be declined. Marketing organizations must educate their colleagues with clear data on efforts that impact outcomes. Until this happens, the marketing team will continue to be activity driven and ROI-measured (Exhibit 9.4).

EXHIBIT 9.4 Operational Metrics

	Metric	Last Year's Results	Next Year's Target
Operationally-Based Metrics: Supporting Systems and Infrastructure	Cost/lead	$250	$200
	Channel margin	5% tier-1 channel	7% tier-1 channel
	Conversion rate	60%	70%
	Program/people ratio Overall Payback Average Customer Acquisition Cost	3.72 3:1 $7500/custome	3.85 7:1 $5000/customer

Metrics that typically quantify efficiency and cost are generally in this category.

Information for Strategic Decisions

More efficient, maybe more productive, perhaps more cost effective, but what information do you have to make strategic recommendations or decisions? Marketing must transition to metrics based in business outcomes. An example of an outcome could be: "Obtain 15% market share in the health care market within three years." How to achieve this outcome will depend on the marketing strategy, whether it be devoted to focusing on a particular segment or going through a specific channel.

EXHIBIT 9.5 Outcome-based Metrics

	Metric	Last Year's Results	Next Year's Target
Outcome-Based Metrics: Business Metrics/ Business results	# share determiners/ segment	One share determiner/segment	Top two share determiners/ segment
	Customer Attrition rate (annualized) Pipeline Contribution	15% 8%	12% 12%

Metrics that typically demonstrate how marketing performance contributed to the business. Metrics are oriented against the business outcomes and generally address acquisition, retention, and value.

The outcome and strategy serve as beacons for determining what performance indicators and corresponding metrics will matter most. That is, the priority for measurement shifts from tracking what a marketing organization already does (activities) to what it should do to move the needle in business outcomes (Exhibit 9.5).

The Next Step: Leading-indicator Metrics

Once an organization masters outcome-based metrics, it is only a step away from leading-indicator metrics (Exhibit 9.6). These facilitate business decisions regarding the strategic direction of the business. For example, if a primary business objective is to increase the number of products used by customers, then tracking share of wallet and the degree to which it is improving lifetime value serves as a leading indicator as to whether the company is achieving its objective and taking business away from the

EXHIBIT 9.6 Leading-indicator Metrics

	Metric	Last Year's Results	Next Year's Target
	Brand preference	In Top 5 for all major segments	In Top 3 for all major segments
Leading-indicator Metrics: Directional	Share of wallet	15% tier-1 customers	25% tier-1 customers
	Net advocacy	10.2	16
	Market value index Competitive rate of growth	Equal to industry and next closest competitor	>100 > industry and faster than at least one of the top 3 competitors

These metrics generally provide insight into the likelihood the business outcomes will be achieved. As these metrics improve, the assumption is that the probability that the outcomes will be achieved increases.

competition. In another example, to address the primary business objective of increasing market share in a particular segment, marketing can measure the impact of initiatives designed to increase the percentage of business with share determiners.

Outcome- and leading indicator-based metrics enable marketers to measure strategic effectiveness, focus on efforts with the greatest impact on and contribution to the company's valuation, demonstrate accountability, and provide quality control.

For many organizations, achieving outcome-based metrics is a monumental step. Others move up the continuum, making their way to predictive metrics. Predictive metrics are based on analytical models, which require a significant amount of historical data that many companies may not have. However, it is possible. People often think of consumer packaged goods companies when it comes to predictive metrics, but B2B companies can achieve this place on the continuum. A good example is Ingram Micro, the largest technology distributor in the world with over 170,000 resellers and more than 1,400 manufacturers. Under the leadership of Carol Kurimsky, Vice President of Marketing, the company has been able to use seven years of data to develop predictive models around three metrics: propensity, life cycle, and attach rate. With a fair degree of certainty, the company can use these models to predict the likelihood of a particular behavior. The company uses these models along with segmentation to help their customers be more successful. Whether it is a new product a company is bringing to market or a new platform, Ingram Micro can use the models to help determine who is most likely to buy or add the product to their portfolio and to accelerate product adoption. The models have enabled Ingram Micro to identify new resellers, increase the revenues from targeted groups and rapidly add new resellers.

Moving along the Continuum

Movement along the continuum begins with an examination of your present situation. As we discuss in the next chapter, audits provide a means to assess where an organization is today, how much change is required, and in what area that change should occur. While a self-assessment is certainly a good starting point, using a third party will provide an objective perspective. Audits are not new to marketing. Marketing and communication audits are commonly, if not routinely, performed. These audits typically examine the organization's capabilities related to strategy and brand. A metrics audit examines the systems, tools, processes, and people in terms of being able to measure marketing performance.

An audit will make it possible to assess marketing's direction. You can tell where it is or isn't linked to the company's strategic objectives, where the company is or isn't aligned with other organizations, which metrics the company is using, the degree of competence within the organization around metrics, and where there are gaps to be filled.

Progress Reports

Regardless of where you are on the continuum, you need to report your progress and metrics. Marketing can measure a never-ending menu of items that consume a tremendous amount of energy, time, and resources. Remember that vice president of marketing who tracked 200 unique items at his firm? He's no longer at that firm. Marketing must focus on the most relevant, essential, and valuable actions, and use these as the basis of its metrics and performance reporting.

You can see how the continuum relates to creating a marketing dashboard. A dashboard provides a visual monitoring and feedback system to track progress and connect marketing to business outcomes. Dashboards provide insight into performance, facilitate decision-making, and align strategy with implementation. A good dashboard maps out the relationships between business outcomes and marketing performance. A key step in creating such a dashboard is to identify the most important measures that will indicate success. Imagine the dashboard as really a layer of dashboards. Leading-indicator and outcome-based metrics are represented on the first layer and presented to the leadership team as a way to communicate marketing's contribution and facilitate strategic direction. Beneath this layer will be the operational metrics the marketing leadership will need to run their organization. And then one more layer below are the activity-based metrics used by the functional arms of the organization. Chapter 12 will delve more deeply into creating a marketing dashboard.

Beyond the Numbers

Improving marketing measurement isn't just about the numbers. Marketing must possess the right skills. Skill development in measuring marketing outside of campaign management is rare. Today's marketing curriculum at most universities includes courses that address measuring direct marketing and online marketing effectiveness, but few if any courses on measuring marketing itself. The responsibility falls to those of us with the passion and experience to model measurement training. Chapter 15 identifies skills and training marketing professionals need to be a part of a performance-driven organization.

By aligning measurement and metrics with business outcomes, tracking and reporting progress, and ensuring that the organization is both competent and proficient in measurement, marketing can take its rightful place at the executive table and influence the organization's strategic direction (Exhibit 9.7).

Measuring Makes a Difference

Companies with formal marketing performance systems do indeed outperform those without. A 2005 CMO Council study[4] found that companies with effective

EXHIBIT 9.7 Characteristics of Effective Metrics

1. **Aligned:** Effective metrics and KPIs (Key Performance Indicators) are always aligned with business outcomes.

2. **Owned:** Every metric and KPI needs to be owned by an individual or group who is accountable for its outcome.

3. **Predictive:** The metrics and KPIs should measure drivers of business value, and therefore should be leading indicators of desired performance.

4. **Actionable:** Effective metrics and KPIs enable the organization to make decisions and take action.

5. **Manageable:** Metrics should allow you to focus on a few high-value initiatives/tasks.

6. **Easy to understand:** Metrics should be able to be communicated across business functions.

7. **Balanced and linked:** KPIs should balance and be linked to each other.

8. **Transformative:** KPIs should provide insights that enable the organization to make positive changes.

9. **Standardized:** Metrics and KPIs should be based on standard definitions, rules, and calculations.

10. **Contextual/Relevant:** KPIs should put performance in a context meaningful for the business.

measurement systems achieve 29% higher sales growth, 32% greater market share, and 37% higher profitability than those without. Also in 2005, Forrester Research polled 176 firms and found similar results in three critical business objectives. These objectives were increasing sales from existing customers, expanding the customer base, and raising customer satisfaction. This year a VEM survey also showed that increasing share of existing markets, growing existing customers, and growing brand value were the top three outcomes marketing was expected to address. Yet, while these outcomes serve as the basis for marketing strategy and metrics, marketing metrics at most companies don't achieve a high correlation between marketing activities and business outcomes.

Move the Needle

Where Are You on the Metrics Continuum?

	Novice: • Make a list of all of your metrics and categorize them along the continuum. • Launch a discussion with the team about how to increase the number of metrics that will better link marketing efforts with business outcomes. • Resist reporting on activity-based metrics to the C-suite. Instead, think in terms of what information is needed to make important strategic decisions.
	Intermediate: • Identify one business outcome that your marketing does not currently measure, but should. Within the next month, identify what you need to do in order to measure progress in the outcome you choose and develop an action plan to implement the measurement. • Conduct a metrics audit. Start with the data you have, define your gaps and create an action plan to address the gaps.
	Advanced: • Improve your metrics competency and proficiency by recruiting/training marketers with metrics skills. • Invest in tools, systems, & processes that facilitate the measurement and reporting of marketing performance. (See Chapter 13 on Systems and Tools for specific recommendations.) • Use predictive metrics to guide business decisions. • Create dashboards, not the usual charts, to report your metrics.

Notes

[1] CMO Council (2008). *Marketing Outlook.* <http://www.cmocouncil.org>

[2] Deloitte Consulting (2006). "Managing Marketing Effectiveness: Customer & Market Trends Are Changing the Rules." <http://www.deloitte.com/dtt/cda/doc/content/us_consulting_so_mktg _effectiveness_15032006_revised.pdf>

[3] Farris, P., N. Bendle, P. Pfeifer, and D. Reibstein (2006). *Marketing Metrics: 50+ Metrics Every Executive Should Master.* Upper Saddle River, NJ: Wharton School Publishing.

[4] Forrester Research, Inc., and Heidrik & Struggles International (2007). "The Evolved CMO." Forrester.com. <http://www.forrester.com/evolved.cmo>

Conducting a
Metrics Audit

As discussed in the previous chapter, performance-driven marketing is always linked to business results. These links cannot be abstract declarations made by marketing organizations. They must be measurable and adjustable according to the needs of the business, and to make them more concrete, marketers must not only measure their work, but be accountable for those measures. To that end, a regular marketing metrics audit is recommended, the timeframe of which should be determined by the state of a marketing team's metrics and its reporting needs.

By conducting a metrics audit you can gain insights into your marketing and measurement capabilities and strategies, and determine that your efforts and investments are in line with business objectives. A marketing audit "offers a baseline for performance measurements and a framework for effective business planning to maximize positive external perception and demand generation."[1] It should include an assessment of the current state of the company's marketing metrics, goals the organization should reach (in terms of what to measure and how), and steps the organization will take to achieve its metrics goals.

According to our research, even marketers who place a great deal of importance on measuring marketing performance do not regularly audit their marketing metrics (Exhibit 10.1).

This remains the case even though marketers and other business professionals have increasingly come to understand the relationship between effective marketing and business profitability. According to the Boardroom Project, "cash flow...is the ultimate metric to which every marketing activity should be causally linked through the validation of . . . marketing metrics."[2] Regular auditing allows the marketing organization to learn whether its activities are moving the needle and increasing cash flow by validating its metrics, which allows marketing to work predictively instead of reactively.

An audit should deploy an objective and rigorous process and provide detailed and clear feedback about marketing's contribution. An audit can be conducted in-house or can be solicited from an independent firm. The following case study details the process by which one company solicited, implemented, and benefited from a marketing audit conducted by an outside firm.

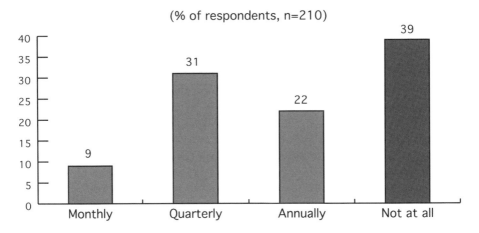

EXHIBIT 10.1 Frequency of Metrics Auditing/Benchmarking

(% of respondents, n=210)

Implementing an Audit

NERA, a leading international firm of economists, took stock and realized the need for a marketing audit. Founded in 1961, NERA Economic Consulting, an operating element of Mercer Specialty Consulting, is a leading international firm of micro-economists that provides practical economic analysis and advice to corporations, governments, law firms, regulatory agencies, trade associations, and international agencies. The company was reviewing a number of their business functions that support their primary consulting practices, including their marketing support function. NERA executives realized that their marketing group's most visible work consisted of supporting its practices with product and service brochures, NERA conference materials, and the corporate web site. In the review process, they also recognized the value to NERA of a marketing function that contributes to management's business development strategy. "Because the company will look increasingly to the marketing department to assist NERA in taking corporate strategy to the next level, we wanted an independent firm to help us create a baseline data point regarding marketing's value and contribution," said Andrew S. Carron, president of NERA.

The First Step

The company used 13 different categories to evaluate marketing performance. Each category is divided into subcategories reflecting marketing best practices. Exhibit 10.2 lists the categories and subcategories.

Based on the results of the assessment process, the team calculated an overall score that was a composite of the scores for each category.

The audit process was comprised of three phases. The first phase included a thorough review of NERA's business and marketing documentation. This documen-

EXHIBIT 10.2 Marketing Best Practices

Purpose	• Clarity of Purpose • Individual Purpose	Goals	• Planning • Communication • Performance
Alignment	• Objectives • Processes • Tools • Communication	Measurement	• Metrics • Dashboard
People	• Selection • Individual Responsibilities • Training • Executives • Team Skills & Size	Competition	• Information Collection • Information Reporting • Use of Information
Customer	• General Customer Information • Current Customers • Target Customers	Programs	• Planning • Performance
Infrastructure	• Systems and Tools • Usage • Training • Marketing Information System • Marketing Planning System • Marketing Control System	Support	• Management • Cross-Functional • Resources • Culture
Evolution	• Plans & Policies • Audit	Investment	• Budget Management • Value Calculation • Assessment
Functionality	• Representation • Abilities/ Responsibilities		

tation included the company's business plans, marketing plans, and marketing budget. The marketing documentation that was reviewed included a personnel skills inventory, job descriptions, training plans, metrics, and dashboard. The second phase of the audit process consisted of one-on-one interviews with the current and past President, the CFO, the Director of Marketing, and select NERA consulting practice chairs, conducted by the VEM team. The third and final phase consisted of a comprehensive on-site review and an audit of NERA's marketing department. As a part of this process, members of the marketing team were interviewed collectively in a VEM-facilitated discussion and were asked to complete individual surveys. The information collected in all three phases populated the audit tool and provided an objective, thorough assessment of NERA's marketing function.

The results of the audit helped identify needs and opportunities. Based on the audit results, NERA's executive leadership realized that there was an opportunity for their marketing department to provide more market and customer intelligence, competitive differentiation, new business opportunities, and strategic market advice. NERA also recognized that, with these changes, their marketing department would increase their value to the organization by increasing the return on their current investment in marketing. In addition, like many marketing organizations in today's corporate environments, NERA's marketing team found that they could benefit from better alignment to corporate goals and rigorous measurement of the results of their activities.

Alignment and measurement are key for any marketing department's success in making the right investments and demonstrating their contribution to corporate value. Companies whose audits demonstrate higher marketing performance have two things in common: They have set specific, measurable marketing objectives that are closely aligned with the business; and they have instilled a culture of accountability in all their activities. "While the audit served its primary purpose of helping us understand our value for money," said Andrew S. Carron, "it also served as a positive catalyst for an internal dialogue about the role we want marketing to play. As a result of this process, we have a better understanding of marketing and a clear idea of how to make the marketing organization at NERA both more effective and more efficient."

Move the Needle
Conducting a Metrics Audit

	Novice: Review your marketing plan(s) and assess how many of the objectives are measurable. Those that are not, review and modify. Interview key members of the leadership team to ascertain how they think marketing should be measured and what 1-2 measures they would like to see in the near term.
	Intermediate: Ask each member of the leadership team and marketing team to independently assess the marketing organization against the 13 categories shown in Exhibit 10.2. Compile the results and identify opportunities for improvement. Develop a plan to address the three lowest scoring areas.
	Advanced: Use a third party to insure an unbiased audit.

Notes

[1] Schildge, G. (2006). "Marketing Audits: Why Principles of Accountability in Marketing Are Useful in Promoting Company Growth." *Journal of Promotion Management* Vol. 12(2): 49-52.

[2] ARF (2006). "The Boardroom Project." *ARF.* <http://www.thearf.com/research/boardroom-project.html>

11

Mapping: A Process for Alignment

Now that you are familiar with the marketing metrics, the metrics continuum, and how to determine where your marketing organization is today, the next step is to create a process that ensures marketing is aligned to business outcomes. We recommend using a mapping to complete this task.

Process Mapping

What is mapping? The American Heritage Dictionary defines a map as a representation. We're going to combine this concept with the concept of process mapping from Six Sigma. Process mapping is a technique for creating a common vision and shared language for improving business results. Mapping is, therefore, an excellent tool for the performance-driven organization because it provides a step-by-step description of the actions taken by marketing personnel as they use a specific set of activities to produce a defined set of outcomes. (See Appendix B for examples of process maps.)

While we aren't so much interested in mapping a process as we are in mapping the linkages, we can still employ the methodology as a way to insure the connections between the business, marketing objectives, marketing strategies, and marketing tactics. When the mapping process is complete the marketing organization will have visual representation that aligns it with the business (Exhibit 11.1).

A mapping approach allows marketing the opportunity to define their own objectives by drilling down into more detailed analyses and metrics to improve performance. It can also help identify skills the organization may need to implement the plan. An organization can use the map to identify technology and training requirements.

Mapping is a collaborative process and generally takes place in a working session. For the mapping process to be effective your organization is going to have to take four initial steps.

EXHIBIT 11.1 Steps in Mapping Process

| Business outcomes | Measurable objectives | Marketing Team Tactics/Activities | Marketing Function Operational Strategies |

First, you need to set some parameters for engaging in the process. It is important that everyone participating in the process understand the purpose. The purpose isn't to ensure that every person's task is accounted for on the map. In fact, as a result of the process, it is possible that some strategies, programs, and tactics might actually be eliminated in favor of new ideas and approaches. This is a common outcome because now that the business outcome is at the basis for the map everything needs to be directly linked to an outcome. If an activity, program, or task isn't connected to an outcome, you should be asking the question of why you are doing it. There may be a good reason for why you are doing something and why you should continue to do it, but the process will create an opportunity to discuss activities and investments that have just been on the calendar year after year as a matter of course that today no longer have strategic merit.

Second, clarify that the map is intended to help the organization determine how it creates value to the business. The point of the mapping exercise is to focus on how marketing is impacting the business and creating value. It is fairly common to see marketing plans that either do not link or only weakly link marketing to business outcomes. One main reason for this is that marketing has a tendency to picture the process backwards, starting from marketing activities and then trying to find a way to map these activities back to the business outcomes these efforts might affect. The mapping process starts with the outcomes the business demands and uses those outcomes as the basis for marketing strategy and tactics, thereby making marketing focused on the outcome rather than the activities. This approach is what enables the organization to begin to transform itself from activity driven to performance driven.

Third, keep the process focused on producing results. A well-conceived map creates a framework that will serves as the foundation for the marketing plan and a set of performance metrics. It will also help define gaps between what the business requires and what marketing is executing. These gaps provide an opportunity for improvement, and the more the team approaches mapping with this in mind, the more effective the mapping process will be.

The mapping process is typically conducted by a facilitator working with a group of people who can provide valuable input to the map. For marketing, this group often includes key members from the marketing leadership team, marketing personnel who are responsible for implementation, and members from finance, product, sales, and service. The facilitator prompts the group to define the business outcomes, the objectives necessary for achieving these outcomes, the set and sequence of tasks to implement the objective, the resulting outputs, and any other elements of importance. One popular approach we use is to cover a wall with a very large sheet of paper and write each outcome on the papers. Then using adhesive-backed paper, we work in teams to create the objectives, strategies and tasks. The notes are arranged and rearranged in sequence until everyone is satisfied that the map accurately and comprehensively links marketing to the business results.

To create a map, follow these five steps:

1. Identify key business outcomes and select those that marketing can impact.
2. Define the initiatives marketing will drive to achieve the outcomes.
3. Establish quantifiable, measurable objectives to support each initiative.
4. Develop strategies for each marketing function that will drive the objectives.
5. Clarify each activity/tactic for each member of the team.

Remember: you want to organize your map around the outcomes and focus on those objectives that enable marketing to create value for the organization. This technique places the outcomes in the foreground, clarifying what the organization is trying to achieve. For example, if a key outcome is sales from a particular set of products and marketing's role is to accelerate production adoption through trial, you can agree that trials are an important part of the product adoption process even if team members have different ideas about how to create trials. With the outcome in the foreground, the team can work toward consensus in the activity steps and group activities by outcomes.

Through the mapping process, your team can keep a constant focus on your most mission-critical outcomes and the primary question: How can marketing create real value to the customer and therefore the business? Everything you do to find, gain, and keep customers should create clear value for the customer and the company. Creating value is the organization's and marketing's number one defense against changing markets, competition, and technologies. The more marketing can help the organization achieve an ever-growing stream of profitable business, the more impact marketing has the organization and the more it can measure its contribution.

The map needs to articulate the specific measurable results. Statements such as "Use our distribution network," "Facilitate decision-making," or "Confirm joint commitments" are not measurable and do not connect marketing to a key business element—the money. Although people will agree that these are important steps, their value and impact cannot be proven. You want the items on your map to be able to be both measurable and linked back to outcome in such a way as to prove value. For example, if a key strategy for achieving a sales outcome requires sales enablement in order achieve the sales results, then there must be a marketing objective and set of tactics that can be measured in terms of both sales enablement and the sales results. Everyone would agree that sales enablement does in fact help salespeople become more effective at reaching their sales quotas. Even so, we need to measure the impact and effectiveness in terms of the investment and payback.

The marketing organization's performance should be measured against the outcomes and objectives, rather than the detailed steps. There are many advantages to selecting metrics at this point on the map. For example, if the objective is designed around generating pipeline contribution and marketing is not generating enough good opportunities into the pipeline, then the marketing strategy needs to be adjusted so as to create enough opportunities. Because products and services move

EXHIBIT 11.2 Mapping Process

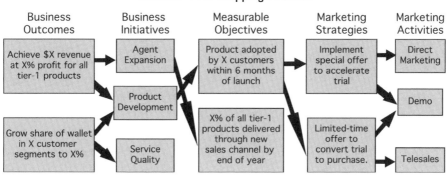

through their economic life cycles, a company may need to change their marketing and qualifying strategies accordingly. If all we are measuring is activity, we will not know when we need to make a strategic adjustment. The metrics defined by the mapping process can provide powerful leading indicators that will facilitate strategic and investment decisions enabling the organization to allocate resources most effectively.

Exhibit 11.2 provides an example.

Start the process by asking the following question: "What needles does marketing need to move?" This information can often be gleaned from the organization's business plan. For example, a company typically has a revenue target and has several key strategies or initiatives designed to achieve the performance target. Exhibit 11.3 illustrates this idea.

The items in the bubbles are the business outcomes marketing is expected to impact. Once the outcomes are identified, the first level of the map can be completed. That is, now that we know what needles to move we can create measurable objectives, strategies, and tactics. The next step is to map marketing activities to these outcomes. The key question to address is, "What must marketing do to contribute to each of the performance targets?"

The four items in Exhibit 11.4 represent four measurable marketing objectives the marketing organization will work to achieve. The process continues until every business outcome has a set of marketing objectives.

EXHIBIT 11.3 Needles

Go from $X billion in ACME Insurance to $Y billion by 2010

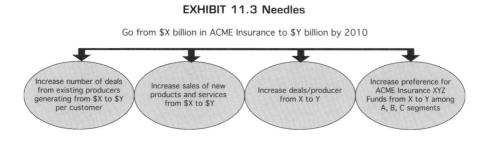

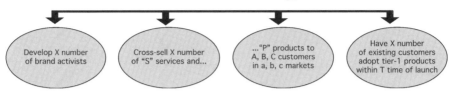

EXHIBIT 11.4 Measurable Objectives

Increase the number of deals from existing producers

Develop X number of brand activists

Cross-sell X number of "S" services and...

..."P" products to A, B, C customers in a, b, c markets

Have X number of existing customers adopt tier-1 products within T time of launch

Once this step is complete strategies are created that will enable the organization to achieve the objectives. Only after these three steps are completed will marketing begin to identify tactics. Using this process, tactics that have always been done, such as attending a particular event or running a particular customer program, don't end up on the list just because they've always been done. Rather, only tactics that actually support the strategies make it onto the map. Because the list of tactics can be endless, it is often a good idea to weight each tactic in terms of the contribution each tactic will make toward achievement the strategy. If necessary a weighting process can be applied through the process. With a completed map, it is easy to spot redundancies, omissions, ineffective activities, and other obstacles that impede performance. Tactics that are not linked up can be phased out. When you are finished, your high-level map should look something like Exhibit 11.5. This map can then serve as a blueprint for your marketing plan and a foundation for your dashboard.

The Benefits

Companies benefit from going through the mapping process. The following case study illustrates the process and its results. BAX Global, Inc., with worldwide headquarters in Irvine, CA, is a $2.4 billion supply chain management and transportation solutions company offering multimodal logistics management for business-to-business shippers through a global network of nearly 500 offices in 136 countries. BAX specializes in managing the movement of heavyweight packages and cargo of all shapes and sizes. The company is a wholly-owned subsidiary of Brinks.

The company previously had established a set of metrics for measuring the performance of its marketing programs, but it was interested in taking these efforts to the next level. Jerry Levy, then Vice President of Marketing for BAX Global, believed a good first step in improving their marketing performance management was making an objective assessment of the company's marketing plan and the metrics and dashboard used for tracking and reporting. Following the assessment, he wanted the marketing organization's goals better aligned with the business goals.

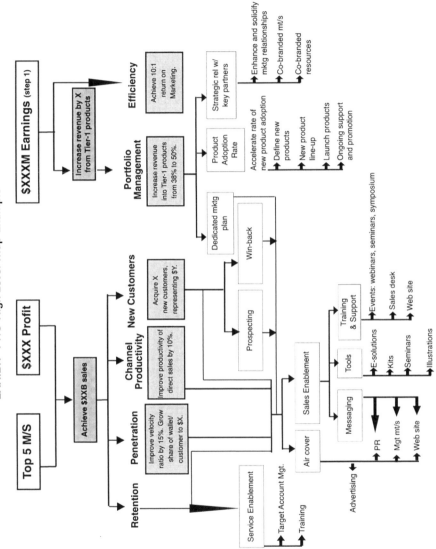

EXHIBIT 11.5 High-Level Map Example

Measuring the Results

Marketers need to measure results, not just activities. Being a logistics company, BAX Global is highly proficient in measuring and tracking its operational functions. Its marketing organization was reporting its performance in the same vein, measuring activities and productivity. After a review of the current dashboard and marketing plan, it was clear that the organization effectively tracked progress on activities and that it had an opportunity to improve on how it reported on the business results of those activities. Levy wanted to be sure the executive team understood how marketing was impacting the business.

Assessment: the First Step

To address BAX Global's needs, the marketing plan was evaluated and scored against a set of eight dimensions. The purpose of this step was to help identify the gaps between and among the marketing plans, marketing metrics, and business goals. The assessment method is designed also to help companies improve their marketing plan's support for business goals and provide the right metrics framework for measuring their marketing performance.

First BAX Global's marketing plan was evaluated in order to identify areas for improvement. Specific recommendations ranged from making objectives measurable to including a discussion of risks and opportunities. According to Levy, "The analysis of our marketing plan was surprisingly eye-opening. It revealed many areas for us to address to make the plans more relevant and understandable to top management."

The Next Step: Mapping

After the assessment of the marketing organization and its plan, the BAX Global team of product managers, business analysts, product marketers, and communications specialists used the mapping process as way to shore up the linkages between marketing initiatives, objectives, strategies, and metrics. The mapping process helped BAX Global visualize the trajectory from business outcomes to marketing objectives, strategies, and tactics. Upon completion, the work then turned to focusing on selecting the right metrics and designing the optimal reporting dashboard. By the end of the session the company had a map they could use to model a dashboard.

The process results in a new plan. At the end of the assessment, BAX Global had a draft of a marketing plan that contained the right balance of strategy and tactics. More importantly, it told a clear story of how the marketing function was going to address the opportunities in the marketplace and drive the business forward.

The project also helped marketing define a new way to communicate how marketing is impacting the business. The BAX Global team now had a short list of metrics they felt served as indicators of marketing performance. A few examples of these key performance indicators and metrics for the dashboard included customer churn rate, market share by vertical, share of wallet, and company growth rate compared to category growth rate.

The company also gained a new method for evaluating and scoring its future marketing plans. Perhaps most importantly, executive management gained a better understanding of the role of the marketing function in the company and how it can be measured.

By using the mapping process, a performance-driven marketing organization can lay out the hierarchical relationships among the:

- Company's business objectives.
- Marketing objectives intended to achieve them.
- Strategies required to deliver on the objectives.
- Tactics needed to support the strategies.
- Business processes to deliver the performance targets.
- Information systems to support the business processes.
- Organizational skills, structures, and culture required to pursue the objectives successfully.

The map illustrates the "many-to-many" relationships between business goals, marketing objectives, strategies and tactics. The mere process of deciding what are the outcomes vs. the objectives vs. the strategies vs. the tactics brings all marketing department activity to the forefront, exposing gaps and inefficiencies for the benefit of continuous improvement.

The leaders of the marketing organization need to generate a common vision and implement it collaboratively. Mapping is an ideal tool to engage people in creating and achieving this common vision. But, as with every tool, there are advantages and disadvantages and it won't solve every problem. The advantage of using the mapping process is that you have visual representation of your plan and a clear view into how marketing is directly linked to the business. A completed process map can also serve as an effective educational and communication tool. However, mapping requires an investment of time and employee involvement as well as collection of valuable data. It also requires a high level of facilitation skills to guide a group through the mapping exercise. People who do not like working with detail may find it difficult to participate in the process. And, finally, beware of creating a map based on the input from only a small group of marketing people. There are a number of resources out there to help you prepare for mapping and conduct a mapping session.[1]

Move the Needle

Map Your Destination

	Novice: • Take your current business plan and marketing plan and map them. Identify any holes and develop a plan of action to address.
	Intermediate: • Working as a team, use the mapping process before you create your next marketing plan.
	Advanced: • Create a cross-functional team with representatives from sales, product, manufacturing and/or implementation, customer service and finance to participate in the mapping process.

Notes

[1] For example, see Marrelli, A. "Process Mapping." *Performance Improvement*, 44(5): 40-44. <http://www.ipsi.org/pdf/suggestedReading/Article-Four_ProcessMapping.pdf>

Developing Your Dashboard and Specification

Performance-driven marketing requires accurate and consistent reporting. A dashboard is a graphic tool for reporting how marketing is moving the needle for the business. A good dashboard correlates marketing investments and metrics, rather than simply tracking and reporting activities.

It is difficult to measure the impact of marketing on the business when the marketing organization reports activities, such as how many people downloaded a document, attended a webinar, or how many press hits resulted from a release. These activities may be important, but the connection to the business is unclear.

The following example illustrates the point. If someone reports that they ran five times this week, what do we know? Not very much: at minimum we don't know how much they were *scheduled* to run and at the maximum we don't know the purpose of the running. If a person's outcome is to lose 20 pounds in six months, then it is very likely s/he will have two objectives. One will be to decrease caloric intake and one will be to increase caloric output, because it is a scientific fact that there are 3,500 calories per pound. A certain number of calories are required to function, everything over that is subject to scrutiny. If these are the two objectives, then a person might deploy several strategies: a portion reduction strategy or a dessert elimination strategy for the caloric intake objective and a physical exertion strategy for the caloric expenditure objective. The activity to expend the calories might be running. So the real metrics are related to calories, and, therefore, while running may be something that is tracked and monitored, it is calories that need to be reported.

If we were to have an outcome to complete a 5K this year under 28 minutes, that running is still going to be an activity. Depending on your current capabilities you may have objectives related to distance and speed. To achieve these objectives, you are going to have to run some number of times each week. Again, while running will be tracked and monitored, the metric is pace; this is the needle you will have to move to achieve the outcome.

Hopefully, the example illustrates why the marketing dashboard shared with the C-suite needs to report on outcomes rather than activities. By focusing on outcomes, the dashboard will provide as much as possible real-time insight regarding marketing performance and progress in relationship to the business goals. In an article on dashboards and marketing, Pauwels et al. indicate that, for marketing, dashboards are related to decision support systems.[1] They suggest three main uses for a marketing dashboard:

1. Provide market feedback in a consistent and coordinated way.
2. Facilitate marketing performance evaluation.
3. Planning.

We believe there are two primary benefits that come from having a marketing dashboard. First, it enables the marketing executive team to make fact-based decisions that will allow them to allocate future resources based on what is working versus what is not. Second, it facilitates the communication of marketing objectives and results—ensuring that the marketing team is in sync across the organization, and that senior executives are provided consistent, relevant data on their progress toward key objectives. Ultimately, dashboards serve as a monitoring and feedback system.

Reibstein et al., propose five stages of dashboard development:[2]

1. Selecting key metrics.
2. Populating the dashboard with data.
3. Establishing relationships between the dashboard items.
4. Forecasting and "what if" analysis.
5. Connecting to financial consequences.

We believe the process needs to include a few additional steps. Once the key metrics are selected, we recommend you create a pro-forma using historical data. This way you can determine the availability of the data and test your hypotheses. Once you have validated the dashboard, we recommend that you create a dashboard specification, which at a minimum defines the metrics, how the metric is calculated, and the data sources. Once the specification is completed, an "alpha" (preliminary version using current data) can be generated.

Just as with the mapping process, in order to develop a dashboard, you must begin with business outcomes. From there you must identify the most important measures of success, define key performance indicators (KPIs) connected with those measures, determine which data provide the necessary information, and analyze and report those data. From tracking to analysis to reporting, a quality dashboard covers it all.

Most companies need a multilevel dashboard: a top level that the marketing leadership can present to the C-suite and that communicates how marketing is impacting the business; a level that the marketing leadership can use to manage the organization; and then a level that offers a view into how each individual function or activity is performing. Exhibit 12.1 illustrates a multilevel dashboard.

EXHIBIT 12.1 Multilevel Dashboard

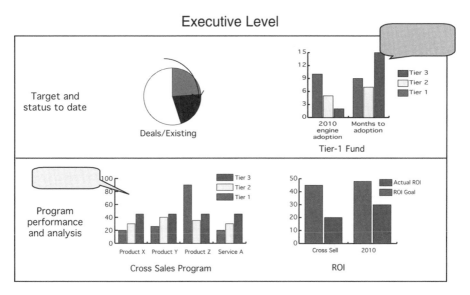

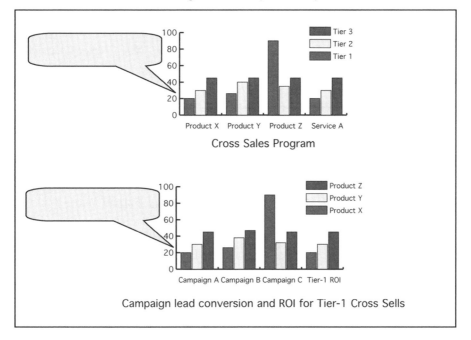

By using a dashboard, performance-driven organizations can identify outcomes where marketing is making a significant contribution. They can also use the dashboard to create tighter alignment with the business and sharpen their focus on the most critical business issues. The dashboard becomes a tool by which the performance-driven organization makes decisions on how to best direct marketing resources to improve outcomes.

Design Your Dashboard to achieve the following:

1. Demonstrate how you are moving the needle.
2. Communicate what performance indicators affect the business.

To begin, focus on the most relevant, essential, and valuable outcomes where marketing can make a difference. Metrics and key performance indicators are the heart and soul of a dashboard, so it is important to identify the critical measure of success at the outset. The mapping process can provide guidance in this area. Once the measures have been identified, define the performance indicators connected with these measures. To achieve these two goals you will need to know what information or data is necessary and whether you have access to this information and if not, how will you acquire the data.

Dashboard Specifications

How do you know what to put in your dashboard? Just as important as having a dashboard is knowing what it should track and report. This is where dashboard specification comes in. Dashboard specifications vary according to business types and desired outcomes, but they should include relevant metrics, outcomes, and responsible parties. The template in Exhibit 12.2 should help you develop your own dashboard specification, regardless of your particular business.

Some metrics categories must be included in every dashboard, including metrics related to:

- New business/customer acquisition.
- Performance against the competition such as share of preference, rate of growth.
- Customer value metrics such as share of wallet.
- Overall net advocacy score.
- Your market value index.
- Product innovation metrics.

Each of these metrics connects marketing's function to business outcomes and provides a clear picture of both current and potential progress in marketing performance. Exhibit 12.3 shows a functional dashboard format.

EXHIBIT 12.2 Criteria for a Dashboard

Date	Date published (original or revision)	Version#	Version 1, unless a revision
Name	Provide the name of the metric.		
Description	Provide a brief description of the metric.		
Alignment	Indicate the outcome(s) and objective(s) the metric is aligned with.		
Dashboard Level	*Executive*—these are the outcome-based metrics and leading indicators that are shared with the executive team that show marketing's impact on the business outcomes, its effectiveness, efficiency and payback at the highest level. *Organization*—this the next level below the executive level that provides the information needed for the marketing leadership team to assess how well the organization is meeting its objectives and commitment. *Functional*—this is the level at which various individuals and functional team within marketing provide the detail related to program, initiatives, and activities.		
Organization	Indicate which part of the marketing organization owns the objective/initiative this metric relates to.		
Importance	Why is this one of your organization's top metrics?		
Used by	Who are your customers for the metric? What processes is it used in?	**Goal Setting**	Describe how you arrived at the numerical goal for this metric. For example, suppose you set a goal to increase press impressions: *How did you decide how much of an increase to set as your goal?*
Implications	How do you use this metric? What business decisions does it drive? What does a "good" score represent?		

Continued on next page

EXHIBIT 12.2 Criteria for a Dashboard (Continued)

Date	Date published (original or revision)	Version#	Version 1, unless a revision
Measurement Frequency	How often is the metric derived, and how often is it applied to the business decisions described above?	**Confidence**	Rank your confidence in this metric, from 1 (very low) to 5 (very high). Consider data quality, reliability, timeliness.
Data Sources	List the data sources required to derive this metric.		
Gaps & Barriers	List any challenges or gaps associated with deriving this metric, including any issues that reduce your confidence score.		
Dependencies	List any other (i.e., not already described in another section) dependencies for deriving this metric.		
Measured by	List all the ways this metric is currently capable of being measured. For example, by time, by theater, by vertical market, etc.	**Security & Access**	Is access to this metric restricted? If so, to whom?
Related Metrics	List any related metrics or variations of this metric that you are aware of.		
Business Rules	Provide a detailed description of any business rules required to calculate the metric. Provide a separate sheet, if necessary.		
Algorithm	Provide a detailed description of the calculations used to derive the metric. Provide a separate sheet, if necessary.		
Data Source and Owner	List data source location and who owns the data.		
Example	Provide an example of the metric, including, if possible, its calculation.		

Metrics and the Mapping Process

Your metrics will be associated with particular business outcomes provided in the mapping process. The following case study provides a good example.

Incorporated in 1969, Zebra Technologies, based in Vernon Hills, IL, is a leading global provider of rugged and reliable specialty printing solutions, including on-demand thermal bar code label and receipt printers and supplies, plastic card printers, RFID smart label printer/encoders, certified smart media, and digital photo printers. With the most recognized brand in the automatic identification industry and the most complete product line, Zebra solutions are used by more than 90% of Fortune 500 and Global 2000 companies. Over five million Zebra printers have been sold worldwide and the company's international distribution and sales network encompasses more than 100 countries.

While the marketing organization was fully supporting the business, it became apparent that more work was needed to ensure that the marketing team at Zebra focused its resources on high-value and high-ROI strategies. Senior management had allocated what they felt was a considerable budget for marketing, and a key goal was to demonstrate that marketing was indeed supporting business objectives, particularly in terms of revenue generation and channel support. In addition, proper metrics could also help decision-makers sift through the many requests for marketing assistance and prioritize activities that most closely aligned with Zebra's sales and business goals.

The Zebra team was already measuring marketing activities; however, they believed that current metrics did not go far enough to truly determine ROI on the investments they were making. "While we didn't have a formal dashboard, we measured everything that moved—from online conversion rates, to cost/sale and cost/lead, to publication impressions and clip volume, and everything in between,"

EXHIBIT 12.3

Functional Performance Dashboard

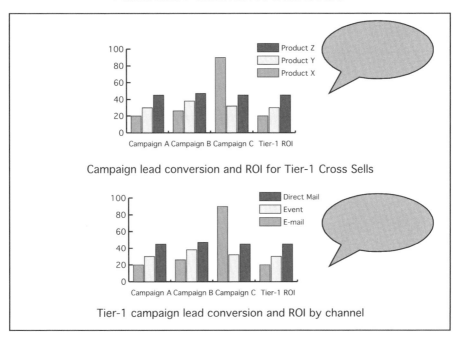

Campaign lead conversion and ROI for Tier-1 Cross Sells

Tier-1 campaign lead conversion and ROI by channel

said Cindy Lieberman, the former director of corporate marketing, brand strategy and communications for Zebra.

Zebra's challenge was a lack of context for their metrics. Without being able to directly link marketing efforts to business outcomes, the Zebra marketing team had limited visibility into how well their efforts were supporting the company. To contribute to the overall success of Zebra Technologies, the marketing team needed to be sure that it played a strategic role and helped drive business initiatives. "To do this, we needed to be able to measure the contribution that marketing makes to the success of the business," added Cindy.

Growing demands on marketing were outstripping the resources, and relief was not in sight. Cindy engaged two other marketing directors at the company, and the team began investigating new approaches to uncover cutting-edge best practices in marketing. "Most everything we looked at wasn't very useful. The approach was to still measure everything, just report on less," revealed Cindy.

The project was divided into two phases. Analysis of marketing and the organization's alignment to business objectives were tackled in the first phase. The second phase focused on defining metrics targets, creating a dashboard, and socializing these within the company.

Phase One commenced with a marketing audit and a series of executive interviews. The audit included performing an analysis of the current marketing plan, collecting marketing metrics, and internal marketing processes. Next, a cross-functional team participated in the mapping process. Product managers, business analysts, research, sales, and marketing personnel were brought together to collaboratively create a marketing metrics framework and dashboard blueprint designed to align marketing with business initiatives and outcomes. The mapping process was among the steps used to support Zebra's goals. In a condensed, highly interactive and collaborative session the cross-functional team was able to quickly align marketing initiatives with business goals, and measuring the performance of these initiatives in ways that were relevant to executive management and the Board.

Phase Two began by creating a dashboard specification, establishing the metrics calculations, and identifying data sources. An alpha dashboard using historical data was created that served as a working model. Once the pro-forma was generated, current data was then used to populate the model. In addition, socialization across departments and securing management buy-in are key components to the Phase Two process. Once the working model was approved, the organization moved into the pilot phase.

"Phase Two required a lot of communication internally. Different stakeholders had different opinions about what data was important. As an engineering-driven company, we're very good at measuring things related to manufacturing and quality. The disciplined, well-defined process . . . was a critical success factor," said Cindy.

The company developed a working dashboard working model in just four and half months. Zebra began to move from being activity and operationally based to being more outcome-based. As result of the process, Zebra began to use new and different metrics, some of which were related to its channel and segment partners—key parts of its business. Other new marketing metrics related to pricing and the revenue form and the number of new markets and applications are in the pipeline. Traditional metrics related to demand generation and brand preference were modified for more relevance to the enterprise.

The work also enabled Zebra's marketing organization to engage in more meaningful dialogues with other business areas, including sales. "Conversations with the executive team have changed," said Cindy. "Not only has this project raised marketing's visibility, it has enabled us to be a more strategic player, to be more than just a tactical arm. The links between marketing and the business are clearer, enabling us to serve in a more consultative advisory role."

Zebra Technologies is now actively working with an executive marketing dashboard that is shared with other business units at the company and is used by senior management to articulate corporate goals across the organization. The company has a clear set of metrics that link marketing to the business. "Now we'll know whether marketing is effective at moving the needle," said Mike Terzich, Senior VP, Office of the CEO.

The project has helped get everyone at Zebra on the same page. The Zebra team is now able to be more focused on organizational objectives and is able to determine which projects to take on and which to reject. During this brief period, the Zebra marketing team began measuring data points deliberately to help inform marketing decisions and resource allocation, became a strategic player and, more importantly, was able to demonstrate marketing's value contribution.

A good dashboard shows how marketing is moving the needle. It helps assess what is and isn't working, shows what is actionable, and fosters decision-making. By providing a unified view into marketing's value to a company, a dashboard enables better alignment between marketing and the business. Just as importantly, a quality dashboard translates complex measures into a set of information that is meaningful and coherent to executive management, which helps marketing communicate as well as track the value of its contribution to the business.

Notes

[1] Pauwels, K., et al. (2007). "Dashboards & Marketing: why, what, how and which research is needed?" <http://mba.tuck.dartmouth.edu/pages/faculty/koen.pauwels/Pauwels_updates_2007 /dashboards inmarketing september272007.doc>

[2] Reibstein, D., et al. (2005). "Marketing Dashboards: A Decision Support System for Assessing Marketing Productivity," presentation at the Marketing Science Conference, Atlanta, GA.

Move the Needle

Develop Your Dashboard and Specification

	Novice: • In preparation for creating a marketing performance dashboard be sure your marketing objectives can be tightly linked to the business outcomes. • If you are not sure whether you have selected the right metrics, make a list of each strategic priority for your company and a list of each marketing activity. • For any strategic priorities that do not have a marketing activity determine what needs to happen to move this effort forward. • Eliminate marketing activities that are not tied to a strategic priority. • Upon completion of this step select 1–2 metrics that will provide insight into how marketing is making a difference and determine how to go about capturing the data for these metrics. • Be sure to include performance targets on your charts to see how your actual performance stacks up.
	Intermediate: • Review existing metrics to make sure they are clearly aligned with the business outcomes. Conduct interviews with key stakeholders around the organization to understand what role marketing plays in helping the organization successfully achieve its outcomes and how they would like this contribution reported. • Identify any gaps between the first two and then use the Six Sigma process to develop a manageable number of insightful and actionable metrics aligned with key stakeholders' needs. • Develop a plan to address these metrics and present them in a user-friendly dashboard. • Socialize the performance metrics and dashboard. • Limit your dashboard to 10–20 metrics. • Be sure to include alerts and trend icons on your dashboard.
	Advanced: • Evaluate your existing metrics against the ideal characteristics (derived from internal and external benchmarking). • Eliminate metrics that are not exclusive to marketing, and thus tracked elsewhere or not under marketing's control; and • Develop a detailed implementation plan with a RACI (responsible, accountable, consulted, informed) matrix to provide clear visibility into the requirements and accountability for each metric. • Create and publish the dashboard specification. • Upgrade your systems, tools, and processes to take your dashboard and measurement efforts to the next level. • Assign individual accountability for each metric. • Dedicate a full-time person/team to the marketing performance measurement and reporting process.

Systems
and Tools

Creating a performance-driven organization requires two key elements: first, an agreed-upon set of standards and processes for identifying and accessing relevant data; and, second, the ability to generate performance metrics from the data. Marketers need systems and tools to implement these standards, streamline processes, and to gain access to multiple data sources. Without these systems and tools, it will be extremely difficult to determine which investments are working and how marketing efforts contribute to the company's overall success. The lack of systems and tools serve as a primary deterrent for many marketers and a key reason for why marketers don't measure results and reflect on what is and isn't working. However, a number of different software programs have become available in recent years devoted to improving marketing performance. With the right systems and tools in place, measuring performance—and thereby creating a performance-driven marketing organization—becomes easier.

This chapter explores the following questions:

1. What systems and tools are important for any performance-driven marketing organization to have and use?
2. How can a particular marketing organization identify what systems and tools it needs to measure its performance?
3. What systems and tools are available, and how can a marketing organization choose from among them?
4. Once acquired and implemented, how should a marketing organization use its new systems and tools? And how can the organization integrate these systems and tools into its workflow and goals?

To help answer these questions we invited two experts to contribute their insights and offer their recommendations:

- Christopher Doran, Vice President of Marketing at Manticore Technology (www.manticoretechnology.com), breaks down the systems and tools necessary for each level of the marketing organization, from the individual contributor to the marketing executive, and what should be expected from each.

- Jason McNamara, Chief Marketing Officer at Alterian (www.al-
  terian.com), discusses enterprise marketing platforms and what
  every CMO needs to know about systems and tools.

Both authors provide concrete suggestions for marketing departments as they identify and provide advice on technology applications that will improve marketing's effectiveness at measuring and tracking marketing performance.

We Can't Manage What We Can't Measure
Christopher Doran

Previous chapters of this book examined the key components of performance-driven organizations. One of these is the ability of these organizations to measure business results and to use these results to identify ways to drive business improvement. In order to measure business results, marketers need a variety of tools and applications to collect data for analysis. After all, we can't manage what we can't measure.

By implementing proper marketing tools, results at every level of the organization can be tracked and analyzed, creating a culture of accountability. More importantly, marketing, once the bastion of wasted capital, can now become an accountable business organization that readily understands its impact on the bottom line and is able to articulate this to upper management.

Here we look at various types of marketing tools on the market and provide insight into how to get started implementing these accountability tools within your organization.

What to Measure

Before beginning to evaluate marketing tools, a marketing organization must first decide what they actually identify the critical marketing metrics are that they want to measure. In creating a culture of accountability, every level within the marketing organization—from individual contributors, to managers, to executives—needs to be looking at metrics in order to refine the work it bases on the metrics. The metrics of interest within each level will vary greatly, and we examine the different levels and pertinent metrics below.

Individual Contributors

Individual contributors are team members focused on various day-to-day operations within a marketing organization, like executing campaigns, maintaining the web site, and so on. These team members need to focus on metrics around their piece of the pie. For e-mail campaigns, for example, key metrics may include open rates, click-throughs, and registration rates. For events, key metrics may include touch rates, engagements, and follow-up meetings. Each of these activity-based metrics should be collected and evaluated in order to decide how the results of the next campaign or event can be improved.

Marketing Manager

Marketing metrics for the budget-holding marketing manager will look at a level above those of the individual contributor. Managers need to gain an understanding of which campaigns work in accomplishing marketing goals. For example, the marketing manager will look at ROI per marketing campaign and how individual campaigns impact the overall pipeline, as well as how leads are moving from one stage of the pipeline to the next, in order to allocate budget, oversee execution, and ensure that the marketing organization's goals are met.

Marketing Executive

The marketing executive needs to be able to roll the marketing manager's metrics into higher-level business metrics in order to be able to identify the impact marketing has on the company's growth goals. The marketing executive also needs to be able to take these business goals and translate them into actions for her or his team, primarily around how many leads need to be generated and how leads need to move through the pipeline in order to meet goals (Exhibit 13.1).

EXHIBIT 13.1 Marketing Metrics, Actions, and Goals

Role	Common	Goal of Metrics
Individual Contributor	Campaign • Response rates • Click-throughs • Open rates • Conversion rates • Leads generated	• Understand campaign effectiveness • Recommend changes to improve rates
Marketing Manager	Campaign Impact • Pipeline contribution • Pipeline conversion rate • ROI	• Understand how marketing is moving leads from stage to stage in the pipeline • Manage budget and recommend programs to accomplish pipeline goals
Marketing Executive	Marketing Impact • Marketing's business impact • Pipeline contribution	• Understand overall impact of marketing on business and pipeline

Keep in mind that these categories are meant to denote ownership. In no way, shape, or form does it imply that these metrics are meant to be siloed by organizations. To the contrary, top marketing organizations create an environment of collaboration. After all, each group's results have an impact on the other players. By breaking these down by group, hopefully you can create a level of ownership and responsibility within the organization.

Types of Applications

As you can see, marketers at various levels of the organization are responsible for different, though interconnected, metrics. Contributors will rely on campaign metrics. Managers are looking at campaign metrics in aggregate in order to allocate budget, while executives are looking to roll all these programs up into higher-level dashboard metrics to gain an understanding of marketing's impact. These diverse metrics warrant a wide array of applications.

Accordingly, marketing applications come in various shapes and sizes. In essence they can be broken down into two categories: individual point solutions, and broader solutions.

Individual point solutions are applications that focus on a narrow piece of marketing metrics. For example, if you want to track e-mail campaigns or pay-per-click advertising, you could track with a high volume e-mail application and PPC tracking applications, respectively. These solutions will allow the team member to execute the campaign and track results.

Broader solutions aggregate various individual point solutions in order to create a *marketing platform*. These platforms are often called demand generation and/or lead management applications. There are several advantages to the platform approach. While offering much of the functionality of individual point solutions, platforms take a more holistic approach to lead generation. Marketing teams are able to automate many of the processes of generating and nurturing leads, enabling deeper tracking and analysis of marketing programs on the pipeline.

Much of the strength of these platforms comes from the fact that they are often tightly integrated with the sales tool of choice—the CRM system. Through this tight integration marketing and sales data can be aggregated together, allowing for more effective tracking and increased collaboration between the two functions.

The downside of demand generation platforms is that, for some organizations, certain feature sets may not be as robust as those of the point solutions on marketing. These weaknesses can often be addressed, however, by implementing a separate point solution to meet these more stringent needs. A marketing organization may need one or more point solutions or platforms to successfully collect metrics at each level of the marketing organization (Exhibit 13.2).

EXHIBIT 13.2 Collecting Metrics

Marketing Role	Point Solutions	Platforms
Individual Contributor	• High-volume e-mail engine • Web analytics • PPC tracking • Ad serving • Landing pages	• Demand generation / Lead management • CRM
Marketing Manager	• High-volume e-mail engine • Web analytics • PPC tracking • Ad serving • Landing pages	
Marketing Executive	• Dashboards • Business intelligence	

Choosing the Right Application for the Job

Choosing the right point solutions and/or platforms for your organization may seem a daunting task. When getting started, develop a framework to help you evaluate and identify the solutions that you need. Key attributes to consider in your evaluation include:

Existing Infrastructure

What CRM or back-end applications does your organization have in place? What functionality do they offer, and what can be added from the same vendor? Understanding this foundation will help you identify how to complete your organization's solution set.

- *Needs Analysis:* As a marketing team, identify which metrics are critical for each group or level. Separate must-haves from those that would simply be nice to have.
- *Functionality Analysis:* Identify key features you need for executing campaigns. Identify must-haves, and separate them from nice-to-haves. Remember, you end up paying for all the extras you identify.
- *Resource Availability:* How much capital do you have to invest in these tools and applications? How many internal resources do you have to manage the system? When evaluating systems, look at the total cost of ownership (TCO)—which includes implementation resources, training, subscription costs, hardware

costs, and consulting costs. Be sure to get beyond monthly subscription costs when evaluating systems.

With this basic framework, begin to evaluate solutions on the market based on how they fit into the solution matrix. If it fits within your needs, look to "try before you buy." With the on-demand software market booming, many players are able to offer a free trial. Take advantage of it, as it will allow you to kick the tires and ensure that you're making the right choice, minimizing your risk.

Keep in mind that there is no perfect solution fit out there. In the end, you'll likely have to make trade-offs. Make sure that they are trade-offs you can live with.

Marketing Technology and Systems

Jason McNamara

The Rise of the Enterprise Marketing Platform

Technology is the greatest corporate asset and competitive weapon the CMO has today. Marketing technology selection and implementation will determine the marketing department's brand effectiveness and program capacity and will ultimately decide the success or failure of the CMO in every organization, regardless of product offering or market. Technology can no longer be seen as a back office responsibility owned by the IT organization. The CMO must own and mandate that the organization create a marketing technology roadmap. Creating, funding, and implementing the marketing technology roadmap may arguably be the CMO's most critical task over the next three to five years. By 2012, if your organization has not implemented an enterprise marketing platform that joins marketing functions and applications (both offline and online), you will more than likely not be in a position to compete and win, regardless of the strength of your product offering or current market share.

The Place for Point Solutions

If one were to create a technology roadmap based on the marketing department today, it would look more like an Excel spreadsheet with multiple tabs than an actual roadmap. Each buying center within marketing would have a tab—marcom, direct, loyalty, media planning, advertising, operations, interactive, brand management, et cetera. Each separate worksheet would have a capabilities matrix that would include a number of vendors and processes to achieve and execute each capability, of course with a budget associated with each task as well. More than likely each tab would have a manager associated with that list of responsibilities, who would likely drive and purchase technology based on their group's desired capabilities and deliverables. This explains why most technology purchases today are point solutions that satisfy a discrete task (such as ability to send e-mail communications faster), versus evaluating technology based on how well it complements and integrates with the enterprise marketing platform. Of course, this integration is difficult to achieve if you don't have an enterprise marketing platform or roadmap.

The Challenges of Integration

It's real simple: Everyone wants to integrate marketing. However, 7 out of 10 marketers today are using at least three different technology applications to perform their day-to-day tasks. Over 20% are using more than seven applications! And these numbers are just per marketing individual—you can imagine, then, how many different applications are probably being used department-wide. You will not be successful at integrating your marketing organization by trying to incorporate dozens of different systems and processes across the marketing department. You need to make it easier. Reduce the number of point solutions, and thus the number of different vendors and processes, through implementing a platform that provides a single interface to learn that consolidates core marketing functions, such as database marketing, campaign selection and management, e-mail marketing and reporting, and analysis.

While the enterprise marketing platform will never perform every function needed, by streamlining all of the core marketing functions, it will immediately increase marketing efficiency and provide the CMO a deliverable towards integrating marketing as well as establishing a baseline for the marketing technology roadmap. Then the marketer can easily identify gaps that need to be filled by point solutions and evaluate those point solutions that will plug into the platform and extend its capability.

How do you select an enterprise marketing platform? Learn from past CRM failures. Fortunately, the CRM initiative over the past decade has taught us many things about automating front office technology, processes, and people. Unfortunately, it has provided more examples of what *not* to do than probably what to do, but the CMO stands to benefit nonetheless. And while this is no attempt to discuss all of the examples of CRM failures, we are going to discuss one in particular—the idea of a single customer database.

One of the promised—but never delivered—big benefits of CRM was the goal of a 360-degree view of the customer, or customer visibility. Yes, the database was no longer going to just be accessible to the Oracle or Siebel database administrator in the IT department; the front office would also be able to see all customer data. But this never happened. As a matter of fact, things got much worse. Companies went from having a single database (albeit only available to trained IT staff and usually sitting on a slow mainframe) to having multiple data marts all over the place, each containing different, often overlapping and conflicting, data. With your CRM training likely came a data model diagram that looked like a NASA launch sequence. Terms like "star schema" were invented, which was very appropriate, because at least NASA should understand astronomy.

Marketers just wanted to see their customer data, and the hope of easy access and visibility into all customer information was replaced with a relational cube, whatever that is. Simple questions, like: "Who are my best customers?", "Who is most likely to respond to a campaign for this new product?", "How much profit did that program generate?" or "Did Customer X receive any other marketing from our company over the last 90 days?" still elude most marketers post-CRM.

The fact is that the marketing department still needs its own database. On second thought, we don't want another database—we have plenty now per previous CRM point. What we really want is easy access and visibility into all customer interactions. And marketers don't think in terms of data; we want information—all types of information, really anything that helps us understand our customers and their interactions and experiences with our brand and our markets. We also want access to our content and marketing assets. In short, we want a single interface or portal that gives us access to all marketing information, assets, and policy. This interface should support all marketing roles and should connect us with our partners and their services. This is the goal of the future marketing department. But how do we get there?

The Future Marketing Portal: A Result of the Enterprise Marketing Platform

The idea of a single interface that connects marketers with the applications (or services) they need and gives access to all marketing information, policy, content, and assets while providing a framework for partners (vendors) to work within sounds really cool to log into. The key to making this vision a reality begins with a technology backbone that sits underneath this portal and connects to various data sources (both internal and external), integrates core marketing applications, provides a technology architecture into which to plug additional point applications, and manages all the processes needed to organize and administer such a platform. So, in order to get our marketing portal, we need to implement a marketing technology platform that integrates marketing services, processes, and people.

The Rise of Marketing Analytics

When it comes to selecting the right marketing technology platform, we must start the evaluation, and possibly end it, based on the strength and architecture of its database marketing and analytical capabilities. Remember the CRM lesson: Marketing needs a database or information infrastructure that connects all data, content, assets, and policy. Don't be fooled into purchasing a marketing suite, which is merely a number of various marketing applications bundled and sold as a package; you will just add to the number of data silos you have and to the number of tools you have to learn. An enterprise marketing platform must eliminate databases at the application level. This should be a minimum requirement for any system labeled as an enterprise marketing platform.

Why is it so important to have virtually one marketing information store? Because you simply cannot have comprehensive analytics without it. Marketing analytics, which includes all metrics—such as web analytics, e-mail analytics, campaign response, ROI, customer satisfaction, et cetera—is the first deliverable of the enterprise marketing platform. The CMO's battle is in the trenches, turning the connected world, and the vast amounts of data it produces, into value for both the company and the customer. The marketer, armed with comprehensive marketing analytics, can now implement dashboards to measure marketing results.

Action Steps

- The CMO needs to own and identify a marketing member or staff to create a marketing technology roadmap.
- To kick-start the marketing technology roadmap and provide its foundation, marketers should evaluate and select an enterprise marketing platform to consolidate core marketing functions.
- A gap analysis can then be performed as needed to fill services with point solutions. The marketing technology roadmap should provide architectural guides for the point solution selection.
- The enterprise marketing platform must provide access to all customer data and a connection to external and internal data sources.
- Empowering the marketing department with comprehensive marketing analytics is the first deliverable of implementing an enterprise marketing platform.
- Armed with marketing analytics, marketers can now create dashboards to measure marketing results and make better business decisions.

It is clear that marketers need to stop adding to their individual applications and work towards integrating their technology into a single system with many levels. Such an integrated system will collect and connect the information marketing departments need to track and improve performance and move the needle for business.

Move the Needle

	Novice: Create two lists. On one list, inventory all of your systems and tools and what data each provides. On a second list identify all the data you need to improve your ability to measure your contribution to the business. Dedicate one marketing team meeting to discuss the findings and to create a plan of action for addressing at least one item on what you need to improve.
	Intermediate: Conduct an assessment to determine which marketing solutions are being used by whom and to identify any gaps that need to be addressed. Determine what adjustments need to be made regarding your systems, tools and applications. Select one gap to address and develop an action plan to close this gap.
	Advanced: Perform a gap analysis between best practices and your current systems, tools and technology infrastructure. Develop a 12-month roadmap that will enable your organization to achieve the next level of performance analytics.

Skills and Training

We hope you've arrived at the same conclusion we have at this point in your reading: To survive and thrive, marketing executives and professionals need to see themselves as champions and drivers of growth who can anticipate customers, develop their organizations' marketing capabilities, and figure out how to measure marketing's impact on the business in terms that matter to their CEOs, CFOs, and the rest of their leadership teams. This will require marketing personnel with a bent more towards the analytical end of the marketing spectrum, as opposed to the creative end. For example, 20% of the 115 chief and senior marketers in a Forrester Research and Heidrick & Struggles study indicated that they need more education in marketing measurement, CRM, and customer data analytics.[1]

In order to create performance-driven organizations, marketing professionals must gain the necessary skills and training to participate in a metrics-based environment. The right data and the ability to use these data are essential for marketers to be able to tap into customer information that will enable them to provide the strategic guidance the company needs to extend into emerging markets and bring innovative products to market. By becoming more skilled in measurement, creatively oriented marketing professionals can gain insight into the needs of customers and understand the trade-offs required to design innovative products that meet customers' buying criteria.

The global market is growing in complexity. Only those marketing professionals who have the skills to leverage data management tools and processes will help their companies maintain a consistent brand while optimizing pricing, placement, and promotion within specific markets and connecting marketing to the business. At the end of the day, these will be the only marketers left standing, while those who don't come to grips with data management will find either their jobs at risk or their organizations being absorbed into sales or other functions.

This chapter explores the following questions:

1. What skills (particularly analytical skills) are necessary for the creation of a performance-driven marketing organization?
2. How can a marketing organization determine which particular skills it needs to become performance-driven?

3. Once a marketing organization identifies the new skills it needs, what steps and resources can it leverage to acquire these skills?

4. What can a company and marketing organization expect as a result of its people acquiring these new skills?

To help answer these questions, we invited three experts to contribute:

- Roy Young, President of MarketingProfs (www.marketingprofs. com) and author of *Marketing Champions: Practical Strategies for Improving Marketing's Power, Influence, and Business Impact,* will introduce three essential skills that marketers must possess.
- Rick Kean, Managing Partner at the Business Marketing Institute (www.businessmarketinginstitute.com), will discuss the need for knowledge and ten things marketers can do to make themselves relevant to business.
- Michael Palmer from the Association of National Advertisers (www.ana.net) will address marketers' need for strong analytical skills and how you can avoid being worked by information, making information work for you instead.

Creating a Performance-Driven Marketing Organization: Three Essential Skills
Roy Young

Good marketers should be good business people. That's worth repeating: *Good marketers should be good business people.*

It seems obvious, but in my experience, marketers too often live in a world divorced from an understanding of how their work impacts top-line and bottom-line growth. That's because typically marketers do not understand how the organization gets paid, do not employ a clear-cut set of repeatable processes and standards for carrying out their work, and do not communicate the impact of their efforts to other professionals in the language of business. Not surprisingly, marketers typically face a revolving door in and out of the company, with an average tenure of less than two years.

Without the necessary skills, creating a performance-driven marketing organization isn't easy. Opinions about what marketers do and how they add value can differ widely across an organization. In the minds of some non-marketing executives, marketing is merely a tactical tool for communicating the company's products to consumers. To other executives, marketers are strategic partners who play a key role in generating profitable revenues and ratcheting up current and future customer value.

Under these circumstances, perhaps it isn't surprising that many practitioners in this unique profession have difficulty articulating what performance-driven marketing is, never mind determining whether or not their team is delivering it. But in spite of these difficulties, marketing professionals *must* be able to do both of these things if they hope to create value for their companies as well as enable other executives and peer managers to perceive that value.

Happily, there is a set of skills that, once mastered, can help you create a performance-driven culture in your own marketing organization, leading to a permanent seat in the executive suite. This skill set is comprised of three elements:

- **Financial Savvy:** an understanding of how your company makes money, including what business model the enterprise uses and where its cash comes from.
- **Measurement Savvy:** the ability to assess and forecast your team's contributions to the company's financial goals.
- **Management Savvy:** the capacity for forging connections within your organization, both vertically (for example, between marketing and C-level executives) and horizontally (between marketing and sales or R&D).

To acquire these skill sets, you and other members of your marketing team don't necessarily need to complete an MBA. However, you may find it helpful to take advantage of workshops or courses in basic finance, the fundamentals of quantitative analysis, sales forecasting, and organizational dynamics offered or sponsored by your company. Additional information and resources that can help you beef up your abilities in these areas are available within your organization. Finally, there is a wealth of books, web sites, and online self-paced instructional programs that can help you delve into these subjects. With a little research (googling these subjects and asking colleagues and friends for recommendations), you can zero in on the most reliable, convenient, and useful of these resources.

But before you begin exploring these possibilities, let's take a preliminary look at the three skill sets mentioned above. Armed with a preview, you'll be better positioned to evaluate training opportunities in each of these areas.

Financial Savvy

How does your company make money? Before you can determine how well your marketing team is performing, you have to understand how your enterprise makes money. That means familiarizing yourself with two types of *cash-flow drivers*:

- Your company's business model: If your firm is like most, it generates cash primarily through one of three business models: (1)

"Margin"—offering products and services that bring in significantly more revenue than the costs required to produce them; (2) "Velocity"—turning over inventory as quickly as possible; or (3) "Leverage"—using your company's assets to create licensing revenue. Within each of these categories there are a number of different profit models. Master the dominant profit model used by your company.

- The firm's sources of cash: In addition to its dominant business model, your firm generates cash through three sources (Exhibit 14.1): (1) customer acquisition and retention; (2) share of wallet within category, or how frequently customers purchase your company's offerings relative to those of rival companies; and (3) share of wallet across categories, or sales of additional products or services to existing customers.

How to determine your company's dominant business model and cash sources? You can find clues in the way the firm operates. For example, if the company develops highly customized, expensive products that require close relationships with customers, it likely uses primarily a Margin business model. And if it invests heavily in customer relationship management, it probably emphasizes customer retention and up-sell opportunities as a cash source. You can also learn more about your com-

EXHIBIT 14.1 Business Models

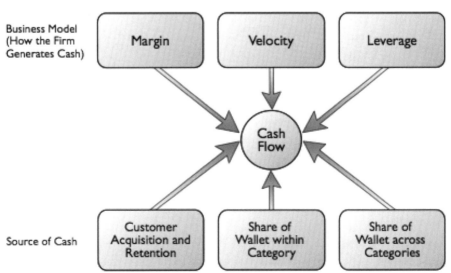

Source: Roy Young, Allen Weiss, and David Stewart, *Marketing Champions: Practical Strategies for Improving Marketing's Power, Influence, and Business Impact* (Hoboken, NJ: John Wiley, 2006).

pany's cash-flow drivers by discussing the subject with managers in the finance department.

Measurement Savvy

What does marketing contribute to your company's financial goals? Once you know how your company makes money, the next step to creating a performance-driven marketing team is to measure the extent to which marketing contributes to the company's financial goals. You can do this through a *marketing audit* (See also Chapter 10 of this book):

> Identify the marketing activities and metrics that directly *and indirectly* affect your company's cash-flow drivers. For instance, if your firm relies heavily on new customer acquisition to generate cash, perhaps you intend a particular television advertisement to produce a spike in purchases of a product by new customers. In this case, "number of new customers" would be one metric needed to measure the impact of this marketing activity, which directly affects a cash-flow driver.

Or suppose you expect participation in a trade show (another marketing activity) to produce a rise in the number of sales leads. New leads don't necessarily turn into new customers, so this activity has an indirect affect on your firm's cash-flow drivers. "Number of new leads" is thus an intermediate metric. You need to forge the final link in the cause-and-effect chain by articulating how you will transform fresh leads into more sales from new customers and thus influence that cash-flow driver.

Exhibit 14.2 provides additional examples of intermediate metrics and how they might affect various cash-flow drivers in your company:

> Test the assumptions behind your cause-and-effect links. To make a credible business case for the marketing activities you engage in, you need to articulate your causal assumptions *and* gather data to confirm or disconfirm them.

To illustrate, let's say you are allocating a major portion of your marketing budget to improve customer satisfaction. But from a business perspective, higher customer satisfaction is not intrinsically a good thing. What assumptions are you making about how greater customer satisfaction leads to more cash flow? Are you assuming that more satisfied customers buy your more expensive products and thereby increase margin; or that they buy more frequently from your company than from your competitors and thus improve share of wallet within your category; or that they buy more of the products offered by your firm and so improve share of wallet across categories? If you were to dig deeply into the customer data, would those data confirm

EXHIBIT 14.2 Cash-Flow Drivers

	Cash-Flow Drivers					
	Source of Cash			Business Model		
	Customer Acquisition and Retention	Share of Wallet within Category	Share of Wallet across Category	Margin	Velocity	Leverage
Intermediate Marketing Outcome Metric						
Market Share		✓		✓		
Leads Generated	✓			✓	✓	
Purchase Intent	✓				✓	
Brand Preference (Equity; Loyalty)	✓	✓	✓	✓	✓	✓
Customer Satisfaction (Rentention; Loyalty)	✓		✓	✓		
Coupon Redemption Rate	✓	✓			✓	
Distribution Charge	✓	✓			✓	

Note: This would be done for both short-term and long-term.
Source: Roy Young et al., *Marketing Champions,* p. 101

your assumptions, or would you discover, for example, that satisfied customers do not in fact buy more frequently from your firm than from rivals? In short, is the cost of creating greater customer satisfaction justified in terms of favorable financial consequences?

- Quantify cash flow over time. After testing your assumptions, zero in on the ones that have been confirmed, and estimate these marketing activities' impact on cash flow over time. For example, will a series of ad campaigns that you're executing today ultimately improve consumers' preference for your company's brand? If so, when will that improvement occur? And how much cash (in the form, say, of a price premium) do you expect that brand equity to generate?

Management Savvy

How well does marketing build bridges throughout your organization? The more you can build bridges (mutually beneficial relationships) between your marketing

EXHIBIT 14.3 The Marketing Compass

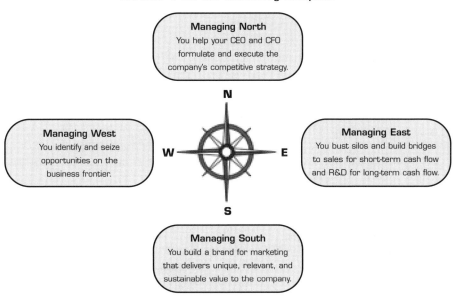

Managing North
You help your CEO and CFO formulate and execute the company's competitive strategy.

Managing West
You identify and seize opportunities on the business frontier.

Managing East
You bust silos and build bridges to sales for short-term cash flow and R&D for long-term cash flow.

Managing South
You build a brand for marketing that delivers unique, relevant, and sustainable value to the company.

Source: Roy Young et al. *Marketing Champions*, p. xv.

team and others throughout your organization, the more performance-driven your team will become. You'll not only create more value for the company in the form of measurable contributions to key financial objectives, you'll also ensure that higher-ups and peer managers acknowledge that value.

How to build these bridges? The "marketing compass" (Exhibit 14.3) shown above can guide you.

The marketing compass suggests ways to increase your team's impact by managing "north," "south," "east," and "west":

- To **"manage north"**: Link marketing with cash flow in the minds of top-level executives through different strategies, such as talking the language of business and translating the outcomes of your activities into metrics that matter most to your company's higher-ups. By managing "north," you build credibility with executives and boost your chances of winning the approval and funding you need to implement valuable initiatives.
- To **"manage east"**: Collaborate more effectively with peer managers in sales, R&D, and other groups by breaking down cross-functional silos, understanding how peer managers' performance is evaluated and rewarded, and helping peers achieve their goals. For example, qualify leads for the sales team,

or help R&D articulate how a new product feature they're proposing will translate into a benefit that customers will value, thereby reducing the significant risk inherent in investing in new product development. In fact, some of the most effective senior marketers come up in the organization through other functional areas, including operations, R&D, or sales, because they understand from first-hand experience how marketing can meet the needs of these other disciplines. By successfully managing "east," you reduce internecine competition and enable your company's different functions to present a unified front—and a seamless, positive experience—for customers. The result? More cash.

- To **"manage south"**: Use the internal and external resources under your control—including ad agencies, customer data, and staff—to build a compelling brand for marketing within your organization that clearly connects the marketing function to cash flow. Then strive to deliver on the promise of that brand by assembling the right teams, developing the right relationships with external partners, and communicating a consistent, on-brand message about marketing to others in your firm.

- To **"manage west"**: Identify and exploit future sources of cash flow presented by changes emerging on the business frontier—such as new marketing information and management technologies; radical practices applied by leading-edge organizations; and innovative services and products offered by marketing agencies, vendors, and other suppliers. At the same time, avoid common mistakes while determining which opportunities will help your team have the *most* impact on the firm's cash flow. Ask, for example: "Which tools and services are affecting cash flow?" "How do we figure out whether an intriguing claim made by an IT vendor or ad agency rep is hype or truth?" "How can we be sure we've adequately analyzed the risks that a new technology, service, or practice brings?"

Creating a performance-driven marketing organization clearly takes time and effort, but the payoff is well worth it. By strengthening your team's financial, measurement, and management skills, you deliver the business results your company is looking for. And you can be sure that, as the senior marketer, you no longer face the two-year revolving door in and out of the company, but will instead earn a permanent seat in the executive suite. In short, you will become a champion for your business.

The Need for Knowledge:
Ten Ways to Become More Relevant to an Profitable for Business

Rick Kean

Professional trainers tell us that everyone needs a refresher course in their specialties at least every year and an immersion in the basics every four years. But, strangely, you never hear anything about any kind of training in the marketing department, do you, even though training for the sales department is an accepted fact and hasn't changed all that much in forty years? And you'll never find any hard data on what companies spend on training their employees or the impact it has on the bottom line, broken out on their P&L statement or in the accompanying footnotes. That's unfortunate, since in a postindustrial age human capital is just as important as capital invested in plants or equipment.

But you understand that, don't you? You've known for some time that your marketing career development is a do-it-yourself project. So perhaps it's an appropriate time to re-examine the fundamentals that underlie success in what it is we do. Our business rewards certain types of people with certain outlooks. Among the generous fringe benefits of what we do are: pride in workmanship, happiness, money, and association with remarkably interesting people. Unfortunately, only a few of us seem to be equipped to handle our jobs with both skill and pleasure. This business scares some, which is understandable, given the number of people in marketing who continue to lose their jobs. Yet, it is a business peculiarly conducive to maintaining a climate of achievement…if you want it badly enough.

Delivering results matters, no doubt. But so does thinking strategically, being persuasive and politically adroit, and having a significantly broader organizational awareness. If we want to elevate our status from corporate gadfly to driver of our company's go-to-market strategies and tactics, we need to focus on two core goals: feeding the sales machine today, and driving the strategic push to define what's next. In other words, we need to be doers, not dreamers.

And, since it's becoming widely accepted that the most effective measure of marketing ROI may just be the impact on sales, marketing should be viewed as an enabler, not part of the power struggle. You can significantly increase your job security by aligning with and supporting the sales organization. The only way to be sure of your success is to be able to demonstrate that your presence is relevant and profitable to the company. To that end, here is a list of 10 competencies you should have that will help you make yourself more relevant and, ultimately, more profitable.

#1: Capture a Broad Perspective

Keep an open mind to the issues that extend beyond your own core competencies. Keeping up with knowledge and seeing the world as a whole mattered a whole lot less in the days of lifetime employment. Today, you need to assume more personal responsibility for the success of the entire company, rather than just the narrow boundaries of your job description. The more you know, both inside and outside the office, the more objective you can be and the more life experiences you will have. Volunteer. Teach a class. Write an article. Mentor a student. Make a presentation. You'll be recognized as capable of accepting a broader role.

#2: Be a Resource

Take on broader responsibilities. You'll kick yourself if you sit on the sidelines. Don't wait to be invited to be a part of the company's strategic planning process. No involvement or lukewarm interest will give the appearance of no commitment. And a strong job commitment makes work more satisfying. It also empowers you, bringing out your potential and making you a more valuable employee.

#3: Build Relationships

Ideas will only get you so far. Count on personal relationships to carry you farther. We have much to learn from each other. Alliances both within and outside the company will be an asset you can use in understanding and taking advantage of whatever changes may come, benchmarking your experiences against the experiences of others. To build trust, invest in your relationships constantly. Don't worry about the ROI. Help people regardless of whether or not they can return the favor. And always give thoughtful feedback. Internal and external team members reflect on you—show them how to win your trust. When things go well, give them credit, too.

#4: Be a Good Listener

You don't have all the answers. And you can't rely on just your knowledge and experiences to guide you. You can learn from others inside your company and from people in other organizations and industries. Learn fast, or get left behind. And learn to say no; not every product or initiative is ready for a marketing investment. If you aren't convinced the ROI is there, don't be afraid to speak up about what's missing. Meet with engineers and developers, and grind through the features and benefits, since it's hard to be taken seriously if you don't have a clear understanding of the product. Reps and dealers and the channel can also be a part of your power base— go on calls with them and see marketing from their perspective. Let them see how you view your job as being all about helping them do theirs.

#5: Assume and Exhibit Leadership Skills

With the proliferation of cross-functional teams, building such teams is a display of management competence. It also shows that you understand the new management priorities, with their emphasis on perspective, objectivity, insight, and knowledge. Stand-alone experts with narrow, tactical skills are not what's needed in today's leaner, flatter organizations. Be prepared to stick your neck out. We are in the insight and idea business. You should constantly be stimulating, provoking, brainstorming, suggesting, and championing ideas to build the business.

#6: Educate Yourself

Proficiency is not enough; you need to become competent. Know your stuff. Do your homework. Either you take responsibility for continuing your education, or you end up without the knowledge you need to protect your career. If you continually educate yourself in other marketing skills, you'll be positioned to take on additional responsibilities. Defend your career by developing a better package of knowledge and skills than the next person. Read trade magazines, attend shows, and track competitive activities. Never stop building your intellectual capital.

#7: Communicate, Communicate, Communicate

Too often we spend money reaching prospects and customers and no time or effort telling our own folks what's coming and when, what our objectives, strategies, and measurements are, and how they can use these in their interactions with customers. How confident are you that your field salespeople have the right story for the right customer or prospect? And if the sales force doesn't deliver, do you place blame rather than thinking about how marketing should be helping to close the deal? Never assume anything about your market—you can't ever know it well enough. Get close to your customers, and use them as partners to pick up responsibilities beyond your in-house capabilities. Finally, you have to sell the marketing function. Spread the word about successes. Let others see that you're for change and constant improvement. Sponsor outside experts to come and speak, and invite all to attend.

#8: Create Credibility

Ooze discipline and organization. Your department is often viewed as the playground, all fun and games, yet posting prominent published guidelines and pert charts for key activities can be reassuring and answer questions at the same time. At the same time, you must continually demonstrate the value of your performance through as many objective, measurable ways as possible. Make a demonstrable difference and hold yourself accountable through continual professional development. Creating a sustainable career means knowing how to balance your core identity with the need for perpetual makeovers. The ultimate goal is to have people think of you, "this is a person who totally gets it."

#9: Understand the CEO's Agenda

Marketers have to align their strategies with the corporate agenda. Knowledge and information, not buildings and machinery, are the chief resources. Marketing activities uncover a lot of valuable information. Don't be shy about passing it along. Get management and sales involved in debating the merits of marketing objectives, the prioritization of target audiences, or how to beef up support for key messages. Tactics then are left to the pros, where they belong. And since you can't manage what you can't make sense of, you must make sure to measure—awareness, attitude changes, rankings, readership inquiries, leads, coverage, hits, traffic, attendance, feedback, awards, and, of course, sales.

#10: Get Involved

Finally, you must be a catalyst for better marketing. Make yourself valuable, so everyone can see that your presence is profitable to the company and that something very important would be missing if you weren't there. Success is not reserved for the favored few. It's available to all who are willing to unlock the power, beauty, daring, and infinite imagination that resides in the human mind and the human spirit. As we've said over and over again, the burden of your professional achievement and advancement are yours and yours alone to bear. Losing your edge is the new career buster. Through access to information, proven ideas, and interaction with your peers you will learn and grow.

It's all about taking responsibility for your own professional future. The great thing about knowledge is that it is not only highly marketable today, but—like your pension plan or 401k—mobile and transferable for the future. It belongs to you, not just your employer. So get it and use it!

Metric Skills: Make Information Work for You
Michael Palmer

Are you putting your information to work, or are you being worked by your information? The issue marketers first faced was getting information; then it was getting the right information. Marketers worked in the dark for so many years—we would look behind them to see where they had been in hopes that it might shed some light on where they were headed. Our analyses were focused on the efforts we undertook, then describing our actions to come. When developing a media plan, we proudly announced how many GRPs (Gross Rating Points) we were able to accumulate and at what cost, with no mention of whether the GRPs drove the business—just that we achieved a $1.25 CPM (Cost Per Thousand). That's nice, but what's the point if we cannot demonstrate the value we received in return for dollars spent?

Marketers can no longer plan forward by looking backwards, by analyzing what happened, determining what worked and what did not in an attempt to predict what might happen next time. This won't cut it today. Management expects predictions, not guesses. They want insight into the outcomes expected as a result of the funds invested into marketing programs. CFOs expect an answer to the question, "What will occur if we cut the marketing budget by 10%?" Before future marketers ever spend a dime they will be required to predict their outcomes, have measurements in place to change or cancel those elements that are not working, and provide incremental support for those elements that are working.

Historically, then, data availability was one of the biggest challenges marketers faced—what data we had and whether it was relevant. This is no longer the case. Data's availability, usability, and affordability is no longer a question. Data are no longer difficult to obtain or manipulate, nor are they very expensive. Technology has changed all that. We now collect what we need in real time; we can see what's happening as it happens, and we can make adjustments as we go along.

But the availability of new information technology requires that marketers once again adapt to new processes and capabilities, and gain new skills, including math and analytics. Marketers must either gain or hire these new skill sets to data mine the influx of new information. Many marketing teams today don't inherently have the analytical skills necessary, requiring them to turn to those with database marketing experience or to the financial services sector, where they live and die by metrics and dashboards. Some organizations are tapping into the academic world to find quant and regression analysis experts. In some cases marketers are dipping into their own financial teams to find analytically-minded people who can both handle the math and learn marketing.

Past brand manager job descriptions included developing and implementing brand strategies and marketing programs for a particular business or product; providing branding direction, developing and executing brand marketing programs; reviewing market research to anticipate competitive and industry trends; and translating consumer attitudes into new branding directions. These abstract, soft skills are out, and hard, analytical skills are in. In this very turbulent time for marketers, there is a growing tendency away from opinion and towards numbers. And marketing managers who don't have an analytical bias and multi-channel orientation are at a distinct disadvantage.

What steps, then, can marketers take to find the skills necessary to strengthen their own analytical tool chest? Read, network, join, and train.

Read

Reading, a dying art, is still a strong learning tool. Hundreds of marketing books are written every year: read some, and find the nuggets of information in each that can help you go to the next level. This book, for example, is a perfect choice for those trying to increase their analytical skills. You will gain insight into finding the right analytical path, but, like anything, it takes time and a bit of work, and it is very much worth it in the end. *Blue Ocean Strategy* has a great example of how to find a new strategic direction: author David Aaker will show you how to brand, segment, build a stronger brand architecture, and manage the complex task of ingesting information into today's brand strategies. Drucker, the master, offers classic marketing insights. And Scott Davis' *Building the Brand-Driven Business: Operationalize Your Brand to Drive Profitable Growth* is chock full of steps you can take to elevate your skills. These are only a few books and authors available to you. Do a little research, and you can find what you need.

Network

Too many people today find an excuse not to go to a meeting, a conference, or a group meeting where they can connect with others in the marketing community. Actually, it is often more valuable to connect with others and find new ways to approach an issue or challenge, than to stay myopically focused on your own business. Using association memberships is a most valuable way to accomplish industry connections. ANA (Association of National Advertisers at www.ana.net) is just one sort of association. Marketers meet in specific functionally-oriented groups, trading ideas, talking through issues, challenging each other, and listening to leading experts present new theories or case histories. Reaching outside yourself is one of the most important and valuable ways to gain insights not available via any other means. And because these insights come from your peers, you can count on their validity— they've been road-tested by marketers just like you.

Join

Join industry groups and attend conferences. Tons of groups provide the means to hear and connect with other marketers. Take advantage of them. True, not all conferences are equally helpful, but most will provide you with the opportunity to gain an insight you couldn't have gotten from articles or books. And, as with association meetings, industry conferences give you the opportunity to meet and connect with those who actually did the work.

Train

Training is the age-old way of gaining new skills. Every association, including the ANA, has regularly scheduled classes, or you can often have customized classes built for your team. Marketers find that they learn as much from each other in trainings as they do from the instructors who run the classes. At minimum, you will be given new templates, formats, or formulas for performing the critical analytical activities that must be part of your tool chest today.

Finally, you can learn on your own. Many marketers seek out their own "training" opportunities by connecting internally with a team member in the CFO's department, the analytics group, or in innovations. Often the knowledge you seek is only a few steps away, but you have to reach out—it won't be a package handed to you like a training course.

Whereas before marketing was not considered "rocket science," marketers are now hiring rocket scientists to help them with the predictive algorithms and integrated databases that give them the competitive edge they need to win. But they are also finding and taking personal steps to keep themselves from being left behind.

Take the Nike approach—Just Do It. Don't be left behind as the marketing world we know and love today morphs into the number-crunching, analytical popping world of tomorrow.

Marketing professionals just trying to survive will at minimum focus on skills and training that will improve their lead generation, pipeline management, branding and customer acquisition capabilities. Thriving marketers will think beyond these variables and invest in skills and training that enable them to grow customer lifetime value and develop long-term customer profitability. As our authors mentioned, a number of different skills are required for the creation of a performance-driven marketing organization. Each set of skills addresses a crucial need in marketing—from aligning with other business functions, to communicating value to the C-suite, to linking activities with business goals. Of greatest importance, though, is the need for marketers to be competent in the collection, organization, analysis, and reporting of a whole host of metrics. Therefore, marketers at every level should be sure to take advantage of reading, training, and networking opportunities to strengthen these skills. Whatever competencies need strengthening in your marketing organization, and whichever route you take to developing those skill sets, make sure you are not engaging in training for the sake of training alone. Instead, focus on those opportunities that will yield demonstrable results in helping the marketing team understand business goals, measure what matters, and communicate effectively across the organization.

Move the Needle

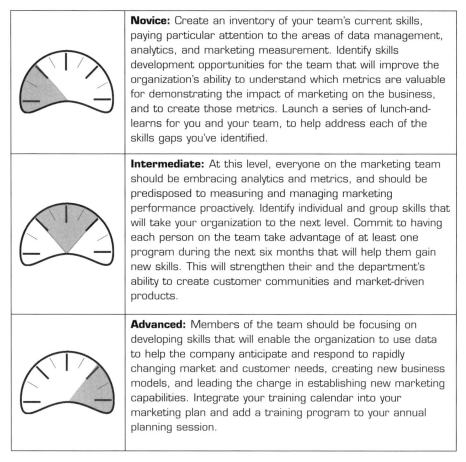

Novice: Create an inventory of your team's current skills, paying particular attention to the areas of data management, analytics, and marketing measurement. Identify skills development opportunities for the team that will improve the organization's ability to understand which metrics are valuable for demonstrating the impact of marketing on the business, and to create those metrics. Launch a series of lunch-and-learns for you and your team, to help address each of the skills gaps you've identified.

Intermediate: At this level, everyone on the marketing team should be embracing analytics and metrics, and should be predisposed to measuring and managing marketing performance proactively. Identify individual and group skills that will take your organization to the next level. Commit to having each person on the team take advantage of at least one program during the next six months that will help them gain new skills. This will strengthen their and the department's ability to create customer communities and market-driven products.

Advanced: Members of the team should be focusing on developing skills that will enable the organization to use data to help the company anticipate and respond to rapidly changing market and customer needs, creating new business models, and leading the charge in establishing new marketing capabilities. Integrate your training calendar into your marketing plan and add a training program to your annual planning session.

Notes

[1] Forrester Research, Inc., and Heidrick & Struggles International (2007). "The Evolved CMA." Forrester.com <http://www.forrester.com/evolved cma.>

Conclusion

"The key challenge is to develop a set of metrics that measure the impact of marketing activities against the goals of the corporation. Many marketing managers will tell you that marketing performance can't be measured. It's not that managers are short on measurement tools, or that marketing metrics lack utility. The problem is that these managers don't know what metrics to measure or how to interpret the results. They may collect all manner of plausible marketing-performance metrics, from customer satisfaction to retention, but if these can't be correlated with marketing activities and revenue results, the data aren't very helpful."

Gail McGovern[1]

I hope this book has helped you define a set of marketing performance metrics that will measure marketing's impact against the goals for your corporation, that is, a set of metrics, processes, systems, tools, and skills that will enable you to create a performance-driven marketing organization and establish a satisfactory method for measuring marketing performance

Let's re-trace some of the journey's steps so far:

- Learn how to measure what matters by identifying which metrics are linked to desired business outcomes, and get started on using metrics to move the needle for business.
- Understand the current state of measuring marketing performance, and identify gaps that you and your organization can fill.
- Create a culture of accountability in your marketing organization that will be able to implement performance-driven marketing and demonstrate its value to the business.
- Get the CEO involved in improving marketing performance, starting with 10 questions every chief executive should ask the marketing leadership.
- Make an ally of finance by acting like a strategic business unit owner and linking performance targets with the company's fi-

nancial goals, thereby integrating marketing into the overall business.

- Align marketing with sales, developing customer-centric practices across the functions that will improve revenue and profits for the company.
- Apply Six Sigma to marketing to provide for continuous improvement in marketing performance by improving its strategic, tactical, and operational processes and grow company profitability.
- Establish a high-performance marketing operations organization to prescribe, implement, monitor, and direct performance-driven marketing in your company.
- Understand the continuum of marketing metrics, from activity-based to leading-indicator and predictive measures. Once you've located your organization's metrics on the continuum, you can start making sure that your work is linked to business outcomes.
- Conduct a metrics audit to take stock of the state of your marketing organization's performance, identify gaps, and begin to fill those gaps in order to make marketing more effective and accountable.
- Use a mapping process to ensure that business outcomes, key performance indicators, and marketing metrics are linked. Clear links drive profits.
- Develop a marketing dashboard and specification tailored to your organization's strategic and tactical measurement, tracking, and reporting needs.
- Identify systems and tools that can automate many marketing processes and improve the performance and reporting capabilities of your organization.
- Determine the crucial skills marketers need in order to implement the changes in culture, activity, and communication that businesses demand from a performance-driven marketing organization.

As a reader, whether you are at the beginning of the journey or a marketing performance management expert, you should have found at least one good idea from each chapter that will enable you to improve your marketing organization's ability to move the needle effectively, consistently, and accountably for your business. With the basic steps behind us, we can begin to look forward to more effective, more accountable, and more profitable marketing in the future.

What will marketing's future look like? First, let's take a step back and look at the present. According to a worldwide survey of 228 senior global marketing executives conducted in February 2006 by the Economist Intelligence Unit in co-opera-tion with Google, chief marketing officers (CMOs) will need to rethink four basic elements of their work—branding, integration, measurement and accountability, and internal organization.[2] As you have surmised by now from reading this book, research continues to reveal that marketers remain dissatisfied with their ability to measure the results of their contribution to the business. Yet every marketing professional recognizes that better measurability is inevitable, given that CEOs and CFOs and other members of the leadership team want to see direct evidence that there is a payback for investing in marketing. The pressure on marketers to be more accountable for marketing results has implications going forward, both for the analytical skills marketing professionals need to acquire and for how marketing departments are organized in the future. Marketing is at a crossroads in terms of whether it will become subsumed by sales and/or finance or stand on its and expand and impact a company's strategic direction in terms of partnerships/alliances, product development, and service quality.

In the near future, marketing professionals within any size company will join those in larger companies in their drive to hone the science of measuring marketing performance and to construct a comprehensive set of performance measures. The marketing dashboard will continue to evolve in terms of sophistication, and companies will employ the measurement techniques of Six Sigma to analyze marketing's impact. In time, marketing organizations around the globe will develop proprietary computer models with sophisticated algorithms that correlate marketing investments with product sales and regional variations and to identify and cultivate potential customers.

Marketing organizations will invest in systems and tools that enable them to figure out the future based on past events and create a set of predictive analytics. Companies will follow the lead of firms such as General Motors who are relentless in customer tracking, focusing significant effort on identifying those initiatives that will increase sales, market share, and preference. The objective of measuring marketing performance is to improve your company's ability to manage marketing assets by providing quantitative evidence for decision-making. This can only be achieved when marketers collect the right data and clarify how these data will be used. The pursuit of data and the ability to transform them into market and customer intelligence is the next leg of the journey as the successful marketing professional gains the ability to answer questions such as:

- Which customer/market segments are likely to buy in the near future?
- What products or services are they likely to buy?
- Which customers are potential defectors?
- Which customers are good prospects to make an incremental purchase above their usual purchase rate?

- Which customers are good candidates to buy a type of product that they have not previously purchased?
- What is the lifetime value of a particular customer?

As we close this book, we can turn to Dr. Koen Pauwels, who wrote our foreword. He writes:

Continuous insight requires integration of data, next analysis, then dashboarding/business intelligence, and finally advanced application. Currently, we are good at measuring the short-term impact of traditional media; the challenge is to look at the long-term impact of nontraditional media. What's next is integration of metrics, behavioral metrics for the upper funnel, and engagement.[3]

We wish you luck as you take the journey into the future of metrics-savvy, performance-driven marketing.

Notes

[1] McGovern, G. (2007). "Fixing the Marketing-CEO Disconnect," *Working Knowledge for Business Leaders*. Harvard Business School <http://hbswk.hbs.edu/item/5764.html>

[2] The Economist Intelligence Unit (2006). "The Future of Marketing: From Monologue to Dialogue, an Economist Intelligence Unit White Paper Sponsored by Google." *Viewswire.com*. <http://www.viewswire.com/report_dl.asp?mode=fi&fi=1091306894.pdf>

[3] Pauwels, K. (2007). "Marketing Accountability: Do we have a plan for research and practice?" <http://mba.tuck.dartmouth.edu/pages/faculty/koen.pauwels/Pauwels%20updates%202007/Marketing%20Accountabilityreport.doc>

Appendix A: Glossary of Key Marketing and Metrics Terms

Activity-based metrics: Measurements like number of press hits, click-through rates, CPMs (cost-per-thousand), and so on. Tied to marketing activities, like running ads, attending trade shows, producing brochures, and so on. While marketing must keep track of its activities and the results, these metrics provide little or no information on the impact of marketing activities on the business.

Culture of accountability: A shared set of behavioral norms grounded in the belief that individuals—and by extension the groups they belong to—are responsible for their actions as well as the results they achieve.

Dashboard: A tool for reporting in visual form how marketing is moving the needle for business. A good dashboard correlates marketing investments and metrics, rather than simply tracking and reporting activities.

Enterprise Marketing Management (EMM): EMM is the system-based management of the entire marketing function, whereby marketing effectiveness and efficiency are optimized.

Indicator: An indicator is defined as a group of statistical values that, taken together, give an indication of the state of some situation either as it is or (if something is not adjusted) as it will be. For a metric to be a key performance indicator (see below) it must indicate some result and/or pending result; this is different from being the actual result. People generally talk about two types of indicators—leading and lagging—and people sometimes become confused about how to differentiate the two. Here's one way to think about the difference: A leading indicator can typically be adjusted to proactively change performance. A lagging indicator usually cannot be adjusted until after it is too late. Try to select key performance indicators that will allow you to make adjustments in both strategy and tactics so that you still have time to affect the outcome.

Key performance indicator: A metric is tied to a target and that provides visibility into performance. For example, a KPI could relate the total marketing spend to the total qualified leads in order to provide the average cost per qualified lead.

Leading-indicator metrics: Measures that are linked to business goals. For example, tracking share of wallet and the degree to which it is improving lifetime value serves as a leading indicator as to whether the company is achieving its objective to increase the number of products used by customers.

Marketing accountability: The AMA defines marketing accountability as "The responsibility for the systematic management of marketing resources and processes to achieve measurable gains in return on marketing investment and increased marketing efficiency, while maintaining quality and increasing the overall value of the corporation."[1]

Marketing measurement and analytics: A collective term for the mathematical engines behind marketing measurement.

Marketing metrics: Measurements that help with the quantification of marketing performance.

Marketing operations: According to Marketing Operations Partners, marketing operations is "a thorough, end-to-end operational discipline that leverages processes, technology, guidance, and metrics to run the Marketing function." It builds a foundation for excellence in the marketing function by reinforcing marketing strategy with metrics, processes, infrastructure, and best practices.

Marketing Operations Management (MOM): MOM focuses on optimizing the marketing function from planning and budgeting, through marketing content management, to global marketing execution and analysis. The purpose of the function is to increase both marketing efficiency and to build a foundation for excellence by reinforcing marketing with processes, technology, metrics, and best practices.

Marketing performance management (MPM): A marketing paradigm that calls for alignment of marketing activities, strategies, and metrics with business goals, making marketing more effective.

Marketing Resource Management (MRM): MRM is a wide range of technologies that can be used to automate marketing processes. The MRM industry includes software vendors who provide the infrastructure to assist organizations with their marketing operations management.

Outcome-based metrics: Metrics that are determined by desired business outcomes, shifting the priority for measurement from tracking what a marketing organization already does (activities) to what it should do (move the needle in business outcomes).

Performance-driven organization: An organization that promotes competition, maintains quality, and emphasizes a consistently high level of achievement. To be performance-driven is to set clear standards and align resources, policies, and practices that enable the organization to hit its targets.

Process mapping: A workflow diagram used to bring forth a clearer understanding of a process or series of parallel processes. Process mapping is a technique for graphical representation of work processes. The process map shows all process-associated activities, including volumes of input and output, approvals, exceptions, and cross-functional hand-offs. The basic goal of the map is to provide a unifying vision of business processes so that participating organizations and individuals can understand their specific roles within the overall system.

Return on Investment (ROI): ROI= (Gross Margin—Marketing Investment) / Marketing Investment.

Return on Marketing Investment (ROMI): In his book *Return on Marketing Investment*, Guy Powell defines ROMI as "the revenue (or margin) generated by a marketing program divided by the cost of that program at a given risk level."[2] Using Powell's definition, if a relatively low-risk marketing program costs $1 million and generates $5 million in new revenue, that program has a ROMI of 5.0.

Six Sigma: A process designed to improve organizational performance by identifying and eliminating defects. Applied to marketing, it can help improve marketing by identifying gaps and quantitatively representing performance.

Notes

[1] American Marketing Association (2005). Marketing Accountability Study White Paper. <http://www.tmcatoday.org/InsideTheIndustry/Marketing/PDFs/Marketing_Accountability _Study_AMA.pdf>

[2] Powell, G. (2002). *Return on Marketing Investment: Demand More from Your Marketing and Sales Investments.* <http://www.returnonmarketing.net>

Appendix B: Sample Process Maps

EXHIBIT B.1 Program/Initiative Development and Target-Setting Map

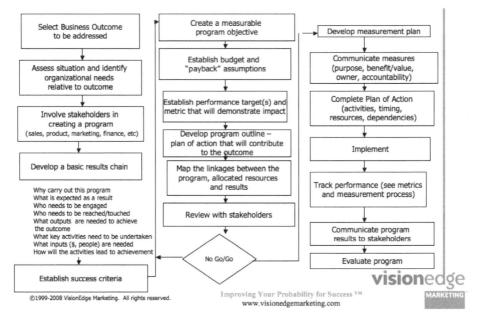

Improving Your Probability for Success ™
www.visionedgemarketing.com

EXHIBIT B.2 Metrics and Measuring Map

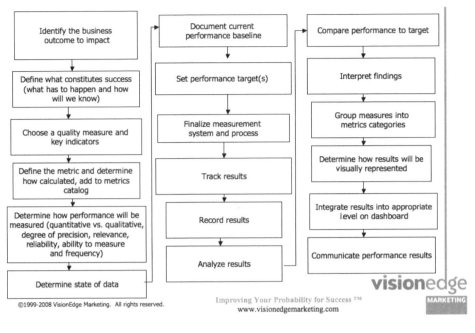

EXHIBIT B.3 Data Collection and Analysis Map

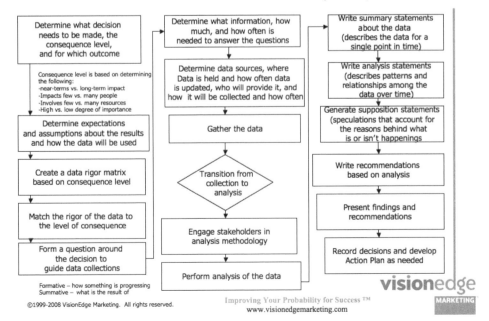

EXHIBIT B.4 Measurement Reporting and Dashboard/Scorecard Map

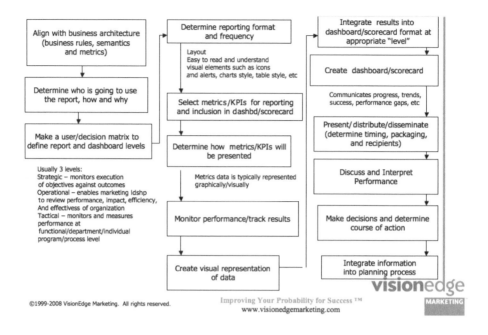

Align with business architecture (business rules, semantics and metrics)

Determine who is going to use the report, how and why

Make a user/decision matrix to define report and dashboard levels

Usually 3 levels:
Strategic – monitors execution
of objectives against outcomes
Operational – enables marketing ldshp
to review performance, impact, efficiency,
And effectivess of organization
Tactical – monitors and measures
performance at
functional/department/individual
program/process level

Determine reporting format and frequency

Layout
Easy to read and understand
visual elements such as icons
and alerts, charts style, table style, etc

Select metrics/KPIs for reporting and inclusion in dashbd/scorecard

Determine how metrics/KPIs will be presented

Metrics data is typically represented
graphically/visually

Monitor performance/track results

Create visual representation of data

Integrate results into dashboard/scorecard format at appropriate "level"

Create dashboard/scorecard

Communicates progress, trends,
success, performance gaps, etc

Present/distribute/disseminate (determine timing, packaging, and recipients)

Discuss and Interpret Performance

Make decisions and determine course of action

Integrate information into planning process

Improving Your Probability for Success ™
www.visionedgemarketing.com

visionedge
MARKETING

About the Author and Contributors

Laura Patterson
CEO, VisionEdge Marketing

Laura is the co-founder and President of VisionEdge Marketing, Inc., a data-driven and metrics-focused marketing firm that specializes in improving marketing performance. Her passion for analytics and measuring value is shown throughout her nearly 30 years of sales and marketing experience at companies such as State Farm, Motorola, DME Systems, Alex Sheshunoff, and Evolutionary Technologies. The author of two other books, *Gone Fishin': A Guide to Finding, Hooking, Keeping, and Growing Profitable Customers* and *Measure What Matters: Reconnecting Marketing to Business Goals*, Laura is also a regular columnist for CEO Refresher and Marketing Profs, and a contributor and Board Member at CustomerThink. She has appeared as a guest lecturer at various universities, including Purdue, Truman State, and the University of Texas at Austin, and at several associations, including the American Marketing Association, the Association of National Advertisers, and the Business Marketing Association. An avid runner, Laura is a Master's and Age Group Winner in various triathlons.

Christopher Doran
Vice President, Marketing, Manticore Technology

Christopher joined Manticore Technology in 2003 to spearhead the company's marketing efforts, including public relations, product marketing, lead generation and partnerships. Prior to joining Manticore he worked in product marketing at AMD, where he oversaw the various product launches that contributed over $600M to the company's top line. He has an MBA from the University of Texas, McCombs School of Business and a Bachelor of Science in Civil Engineering from the University of New Hampshire.

Richard I. Kean, CBC
Managing Partner, Business Marketing Institute
Associate Director, Institute for the Study of Business Markets

Rick Kean has spent his entire career in business-to-business marketing and communications. In 2005, he created the Business Marketing Institute, a web-based skills assessment, self-directed skills building and certification program for business-to-business marketers and marketing communicators. At the Institute for the Study of Business Markets (ISBM), he works to improve the practice of business-to-business marketing by providing a select number of major corporations with access to the knowledge, tools, techniques and resources necessary for success in business-to-business marketing. Rick has an extensive background in business- and marketing-related publishing, including 15 years with Crain Communications and as the VP/Publisher of *Business Marketing*. He served as the Group Publisher of the American Marketing Association publications and was responsible for all AMA published products, including *Marketing News, Marketing Research,* the *Journal of Marketing,* the *Journal of Marketing Research,* and a number of academic texts, newsletters, books, conference proceedings, and directories. There he launched two new publishing properties, *Marketing Management* and *Marketing Executive Report.* Following his time at AMA, Rick joined the Board of Directors of the Business/Professional Advertising Association in 1982, becoming Executive Director in 1992. He then continued at the helm of the B/PAA's successor organization, the Business Marketing Association, until 2006. For career contributions to business-to-business marketing, Rick has received the G.D. Crain, Jr. Award from the Business Marketing Association. He has also earned the Certified Business Communicator credential, a professional designation recognizing knowledge and professional conduct in the field of business-to-business marketing and communications.

Jason McNamara
Chief Marketing Officer, Alterian

Jason has been building high performance teams to create and implement innovative marketing solutions for over a decade. Since being appointed Alterian's first CMO in January of 2007, Jason has helped Alterian rapidly expand its technology platform, partner channels, and market share.   Jason and his team are responsible for Alterian's global marketing strategy including brand, product, and communications. Prior to merging with Alterian, Jason was the CEO of Dynamics Direct, Inc., developers of Dynamic Messenger™, the first enterprise-class email relationship management platform built on the Microsoft ®.Net Framework. Before DDI, Jason managed the Digital Markets Practice for Cambridge Technology Partners (acquired by Novell) as well as served as Vice President at Firstlogic, Inc. (acquired by Business Objects) where he helped companies such as Cabela's, Epsilon, Informatica, Siebel, and the USPS implement database marketing, data quality, and postal automation solutions. Jason is a member of the CMO Council and serves on numerous industry organizations including the Direct Marketing Association's Marketing Technology Council advisory board.

Michael Palmer
Executive Vice President, Member Relations, Association of National Advertisers

Michael joined ANA in September 1995, after an extensive packaged goods marketing career. He gained wide-ranging experience as a product manager at General Foods and Borden; new products specialist at Anheuser-Busch; and vice president, marketing at Martlet Importing Company (Molson Beer). Following a stint on the agency side, where Michael was responsible for the Nestlé Frozen Novelties, Borden Snack Foods, and Citibank accounts, he joined the ANA. He is currently responsible for strengthening relationships with member companies, broadening the membership base and business development. Michael has an MBA. from InterAmerican University, a degree he earned while serving as an officer in the U.S. Navy and a B.S. in marketing from Wharton School of Business, University of Pennsylvania.

Roy Young
President, MarketingProfs

Roy is dedicated to the mission of strengthening the business impact of marketing in organizations worldwide. He is the President of MarketingProfs, a global cutting-edge learning organization that specializes in providing strategic and tactical marketing know-how to over 300,000 members, from entrepreneurial start-ups to Fortune 500 organizations. He is the co-author of *Marketing Champions: Practical Strategies for Improving Marketing's Power, Influence, and Business Impact* (John Wiley & Sons, 2006), which examines the role of marketing within the organization and its impact on the bottom line, and has received praise from leading marketing thought leaders including Philip Kotler, Seth Godin and Jack Trout as well as renowned leadership guru Warren Bennis. Roy has worked with numerous marketers from leading companies such as Microsoft, Wells Fargo, and Visa, improving both the stature and value of marketing within these organizations using the principles detailed in his book. He is a regular presenter at leading marketing organizations including the American Marketing Association, the Business Marketing Association, the Direct Marketing Association, the Institute for International Research, and the Marketing Executives Networking Group, as well as at various universities, including The Marketing Institute at Emory University, University of Southern California, University of California at Los Angeles, and the Claremont Graduate School of Business. Roy has held high-level marketing and consulting positions at such companies as Time, Inc. and Yankelovich & Partners, and he holds an MBA in marketing from the Stern School of Business at New York University.

Index

Racom Communications Order Form

QUANTITY	TITLE	PRICE	AMOUNT
_____	*Marketing Metrics In Action,* **Laura Patterson**	$24.95	_____
_____	The *IMC Handbook,* **J. Stephen Kelly/Susan K. Jones**	$49.95	_____
_____	*Print Matters: How to Write Good Advertising,* **Randall Hines/Robert Lauterborn**	$27.95	_____
_____	*The Business of Database Marketing,* **Richard N. Tooker**	$49.95	_____
_____	*Customer Churn, Retention, and Profitability,* **Arthur Middleton Hughes**	$44.95	_____
_____	*Data-Driven Business Models,* **Alan Weber**	$49.95	_____
_____	*Creative Strategy in Direct & Interactive Marketing,* **Susan K. Jones**	$49.95	_____
_____	*Branding Iron,* **Charlie Hughes/William Jeanes**	$27.95	_____
_____	*Managing Sales Leads,* **James Obermayer**	$39.95	_____
_____	*Creating the Marketing Experience,* **Joe Marconi**	$49.95	_____
_____	*Coming to Concurrence,* **J. Walker Smith/Ann Clurman/Craig Wood**	$34.95	_____
_____	*Brand Babble: Sense and Nonsense about Branding,* **Don E. Schultz/Heidi F. Schultz**	$24.95	_____
_____	*The New Marketing Conversation,* **Donna Baier Stein/Alexandra MacAaron**	$34.95	_____
_____	*Trade Show and Event Marketing,* **Ruth Stevens**	$59.95	_____
_____	*Sales & Marketing 365,* **James Obermayer**	$17.95	_____
_____	*Accountable Marketing,* **Peter J. Rosenwald**	$59.95	_____
_____	*Contemporary Database Marketing,* **Martin Baier/Kurtis Ruf/G. Chakraborty**	$89.95	_____
_____	*Catalog Strategist's Toolkit,* **Katie Muldoon**	$59.95	_____
_____	*Marketing Convergence,* **Susan K. Jones/Ted Spiegel**	$34.95	_____
_____	*High-Performance Interactive Marketing,* **Christopher Ryan**	$39.95	_____
_____	*Public Relations: The Complete Guide,* **Joe Marconi**	$49.95	_____
_____	*The Marketer's Guide to Public Relations,* **Thomas L. Harris/Patricia T. Whalen**	$39.95	_____
_____	*The White Paper Marketing Handbook,* **Robert W. Bly**	$39.95	_____
_____	*Business-to-Business Marketing Research,* **Martin Block/Tamara Block**	$69.95	_____
_____	*Hot Appeals or Burnt Offerings,* **Herschell Gordon Lewis**	$24.95	_____
_____	*On the Art of Writing Copy,* **Herschell Gordon Lewis**	$34.95	_____
_____	*Open Me Now,* **Herschell Gordon Lewis**	$21.95	_____
_____	*Marketing Mayhem,* **Herschell Gordon Lewis**	$39.95	_____
_____	*Asinine Advertising,* **Herschell Gordon Lewis**	$22.95	_____
_____	*The Ultimate Guide To Purchasing Website, Video, Print & Other Creative Services,* **Bobbi Balderman**	$18.95	_____

FORTHCOMING—Reserve your copy now. Send no money. We'll notify you when your copy is off the press.

QUANTITY	TITLE	PRICE	AMOUNT
_____	Debra Wilson Elllis, *Multichannel Marketing*	$39.95	_____
_____	Arthur Hughes, *Successful Email Marketing Methods*	$59.95	_____
_____	John Goodman, *Retail Database Marketing*	$49.95	_____
_____	Theresa Kushner/Maria Villar, *Managing Your Business Data: From Chaos to Confidence*	$49.95	_____
_____	Don Schultz/Reg Price, *Reliability Rules*	$29.95	_____
_____	Weber/Sander/van Boel, *Marketing Triggers*	$39.95	_____

Name/Title _____

Company _____

Street Address _____

City/State/Zip _____

Email _____ Phone _____

Subtotal _____

8.65% Tax _____

Shipping & Handling _____
$7.00 for first book; $1.00
for each additional book.

TOTAL ____

Credit Card: ☐ VISA ☐ MasterCard ☐ American Express ☐ Discover

Number _____ Exp. ____

☐ Check or money order enclosed (payable to Racom Communications in U.S. dollars drawn on a U.S. bank)

Signature _____